DEATH VALLEY ULTRAS: THE COMPLETE CREWING GUIDE

By Theresa Daus-Weber and Denise Jones

With Foreword by Ben Jones

First Edition

Self-published Littleton, CO/Lone Pine, CA

Self-published Littleton, CO/Lone Pine, CA
 First edition 2006
Printed in the United States
1-59971-688-7

Cover photo by Ben Jones
Cover design by Marcia J. Popp

Table of Contents

Tables

Figures

Foreword by Ben Jones

This guide pertains to only a small group of athletes who train for and race in Death Valley ultras. Since the solo efforts beginning in 1977 starting from the lowest spot in the Western Hemisphere to the highest place in the Continental United States runners have been attracted to the challenge of Death Valley. Runners can experience Death Valley by completing a Death Valley ultra in a formal race or a solo ultra.

Death Valley ultras involves three extremes all within the 146 miles of a Death Valley ultra: 1) temperature differences of over 100 degrees with possibly over 130 degrees F in Death Valley to below freezing at the top of Mt Whitney; 2) distance such as five consecutive marathons to the Portals and six consecutive marathons for summiting; and 3) altitude gain of 20,000 feet to the top of Mt Whitney. This guide helps athletes and their crew members plus family members, newbies, and groupies successfully train for completing this arduous task.

Death Valley is important to Denise and me. We have been involved in Death Valley sports adventures since the early 1990s starting as observers. Denise and I have completed the course each three times in official races and have been involved with the competitors one way or another over 15 years. We live on the course at the 122-mile-mark and I have spent at least 2 years, a day-at-a-time, in Death Valley. Our home is in the town at the foot of Mt. Whitney. From my a satellite medical office on the ultra course across from the Furnace Creek Inn from 1965 to 1990, I have been fully aware of the conditions and dangers that can happen in these desert and mountain environments.

The contributors to this guide offer readers their years of knowledge, insight, and experience. Theresa Daus-Weber is a retired ultrarunner and technical writer familiar with the course, its history, and Death Valley having crewed Death Valley ultras 10 times. Matt Frederick is a graphic designer and was the Race Director of Hi Tec Sports USA from the mid 1990s thru 1999. Denise is known as the "Blister Queen" for her talent in treating and preventing skin problems especially of the feet. She has crewed for runners on their quests in Death Valley more than 12 times. I have had the pleasure of living in this area as a practicing physician for over 43 years and participating in Death Valley Ultras for over 15 years. Being a gadget kind of guy, I developed several charts that should be helpful, some articles for comic relief such and staying "sub-barf" and "sub-blister," and information on the medical conditions that can occur.

I hope you enjoy this publication and find it helpful in a successful extreme adventure in Death Valley.

Sincerely,

Ben Jones, Mayor of Badwater

Preface by Authors

From a practical logistical standpoint, which is the point of the *Death Valley Ultras: The Complete Crewing Guide*, endurance desert events are a basic endeavor despite new sports technology developments. The concept of protection, hydration, and heat management haven't changed much in centuries although there are some modern technological improvements such as ice and coolers in recent decades to make crewing a desert event more convenient, safe, and faster.

This guide presents the information about crewing ultrarunning events in Death Valley because for the best success of the runner's event it's as important for crew to be trained to crew as it is for the runners to train to run the 135 miles between Badwater in Death Valley to the Portals of Mt Whitney. This topic of Badwater crew training was discussed on the ultralist, a monitored electronic forum for ultrarunning topics. Discussions concluded that crew need to understand what it means to crew Death Valley ultra runs and be trained to crew it.

This is the reason this guide is written and because we responded to Mike Henebry's challenge for someone to decide to write a book on this topic. Mike's "Running Badwater" that was posted in May 2005 on the ultralist includes information to runners about training as well as information about crewing. We consider Mike's work as the pioneer publication in this niche genre and wrote this guide to compile the pieces of information available in various media and provide consolidated, consistent, focused, comprehensive crewing information in one source. We believed that the decades of Death Valley ultras crewing experience that we have should be compiled and organized to be available for those who want to have as efficient, safe, and successful Death Valley ultra as good crewing can provide.

The baseline information present in this guide is a compilation of Denise's three Badwater race finishes, and a combined total of Denise and Theresa's 22 times crewing, planning, and/or pacing Death Valley ultras events including two double crossings, multiple solo Death Valley crossings, and crewing and pacing the record 160-mile south to north crossing of the Death Valley National Park with only one DNF. The guide also includes the valuable input from Matt Fredrick, the race director of the Hi Tech Badwater 135 from 1995 to 1999 who provides his experience in managing hundreds of Death Valley ultra runners to successful finishers. We have participated in these events because we are intrigued by athletes who decide to challenge themselves in Death Valley and we want to contribute to their success, health, and their comfort to the degree that comfort is achievable in a 135-mile event in Death Valley in the summer. In addition to our first hand knowledge and experience, this guide includes information from various experts and resources and these have been identified throughout the guide.

This guide addresses the practical logistics of crews supporting athletes who have decided to commit to that challenge. This guide provides the information to successfully crew a runner through a Death Valley ultra. Good luck to crews and their runners and have a well-planned, efficient, successful Death Valley ultrarun!

Denise and Theresa

A Note From Matt

I wish all the runners, crewpersons, and support staff the very best experience. Death Valley is a most unique place and can really get under your skin. I hope your experience in the desert will be as enjoyable and rewarding as mine was.

Matt

Chapter 1 — Introduction

Death Valley Ultras: The Complete Crewing Guide is a straightforward presentation of information for optimal crewing a successful Death Valley ultra regardless of the runner's pace. For a runner who finishes a Death Valley ultra in less than 30 hours, there is less to plan, manage, and implement than for a runner who finishes in 60 hours. So the calculations for amounts of water, ice, gasoline, gear, scheduling, etc increase in importance the longer the runner is running a Death Valley ultra. There is an enormous amount of logistics to plan and implement to crew a Death Valley ultra. Whether a runner is crossing Death Valley in an official event or an assisted solo, good crew are essential to the runner's success.

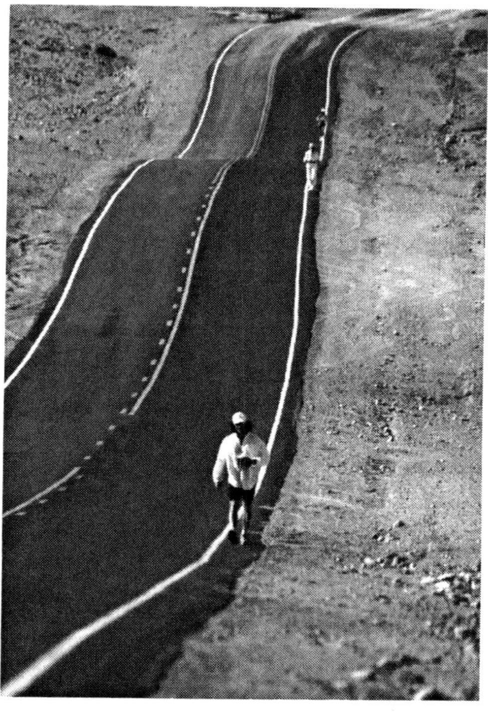

To be recognized as an official crossing, ultras must be completed during the hottest time in Death Valley — July 1 through August 31.

Crewing success is getting the runner to her/his finish goal on time and as healthy as manageable for the circumstances the event presents. Successfully crewing a Death Valley ultra is a balance of efficiency in a confined space of a small van traveling 135 miles through a demanding, changing environment to support the runner's goal. This success is achieved with the combination of four important characteristics.

1. Informed planning and uncommonly good organization are primary to achieve the goal of finishing a Death Valley ultra. Planning for and organizing the amount of gear and supplies are critical. Unfortunately organization isn't linear with many concurrent tasks requiring an ability to multitask depending on the three other characteristics.
2. Flexibility ensures that no matter how clearly the runner and crew understand the guidelines in this guide and how well they are implemented, the Death Valley ultra always presents unplanned circumstances. So, for a successful

Death Valley ultra, plan to be flexible to manage unplanned circumstances. The ability to manage unplanned circumstances requires the characteristic of understanding the elements, the dependencies among changing elements, and quick critical thinking.

3. Understanding and quick critical thinking allow crew members to plan for and solve unplanned circumstances that arise among the numerous variables of a Death Valley ultra to make good decisions quickly.
4. A true understanding of the runner's Death Valley ultra goal and the venue produce the planning, organization that produce decisions to make a Death Valley ultra a success.

This chapter orients Death Valley ultra runners and crew to Death Valley, the ultra course, and the topics covered in the chapters of the guide in the following sections:

- 1.1 Who The Guide Is For
- 1.2 About Death Valley
- 1.3 About The Death Valley Ultra Course
- 1.4 What Is In the Guide

1.1 Who This Guide Is For

The crewing information in this guide can be used by runners and crew working as a team to plan a Death Valley ultra before they leave for the desert. It includes identifying the characteristics that make a successful Death Valley ultra crew member, selecting crew members from family and friends, and considerations for selecting vehicles, gear, and pacers. The guide presents information about crewing responsibilities before the event such as attending mandatory pre-event meeting for official events and preparing the crew vehicle. The "glamorous" part of crewing and the part most people think of when they think about crewing--crewing during the event is discussed in this guide. And the part of crewing that is rarely thought about and planned for—after the event crewing responsibilities are identified. The information in this guide is separate from the information that an official Death Valley ultra event provides to runners and crew.

A Death Valley ultra is a high-risk event in an extreme environment. All the miles and time of the ultra increases the variables of risk. This guide cannot make the runner and crew safe from that risk. Risk is associated with reward and it is the runner's and crew's responsibility to make safe, smart decision to get the reward of a Death Valley ultra finish. This guide provides information to make good smart decisions.

1.2 About Death Valley

The character of Death Valley is as changing as it is unique. From the lowest point in the western hemisphere through three points above 5,000 on its way to the finish at the end of Mt Whitney Portals Road, the highest point in the continental United States, the Death Valley ultra has many unique features that runners and crew can use to gage progress and derive motivation. Temperatures alone change nearly from an average of 125 F on the floor of Death Valley to the summit of Mt Whitney where the average night time temperature is 30 degrees F. The milestones to look for along the course are listed in Table 1. The Death Valley ultra course map is shown in Figure 1.

Table 1 — Death Valley Ultra Milestones Description

Location	Mile	Elevation in Feet
Badwater	0	-282
Telescope Peak Sign on left	1.8	-200
Wide Shoulder on right	3.1	-200
Natural Bridge on right	3.5	-170
Devil's Golf Course on left	5.5	-165
Artist's Drive entry on right	7.9	-165
West Side Road on left	10.5	-70
Artist's Drive exit on right	11.6	-70
Mushroom Rock on right	12.9	-170
Golden Canyon on right	14.4	-165
State Highway 190 & 178 – go left	16.4	0
Furnace Creek Ranch	17.4	-165
Chevron Gas station and ice on left	17.6	-165
Visitor's Center on left	17.7	-170
Harmony Borax Works on left	19.0	-170
Cow Creek on right	20.7	-170
1st Marathon	26.2	-170
Beatty, NV turnoff on right	28.3	-165
Salt Creek turnoff on left	30.7	-165
Sea Level sign on left	31.9	0
Scotty's Castle turnoff on right	34.7	-130
Sea Level sign on left	35.2	0
Sand Dunes turnoff on right	35.8	0
Devil's Cornfield sign on right	36.1	-80
Sand Dunes on right	39.9	0
Stovepipe Wells Village	41.9	0
Mosaic Canyon turnoff on left	42.1	5

Location	Mile	Elevation in Feet
1000’ elevation sign	46.6	1,000
2000’ elevation sign	50.5	2,000
Wild Rose turnoff on left	51.0	2,500
2nd Marathon	52.4	2800
3000’ elevation sign on left	53.3	3,000
4000’ elevation sign on left	55.7	4,000
2nd Radiator Water Tank on right.	58.5	4,900
Townes Pass summit	58.7	4,965
4000’ elevation sign on right	61.5	4,000
Vista Point (view of Mt Whitney)	62.2	3,500
3000’ elevation sign on left	63.8	3,000
2000’ elevation sign on left	66.1	2,000
Adopt-a-Highway sign on right	67.7	1,800
Panamint lake bed, east edge	68.1	1,640
Panamint lake bed, west edge	69.1	1,640
Trona turnoff on left	69.8	1,750
Panamint Springs Resort	72.3	1,970
2000’ elevation sign on left	72.9	2,000
Darwin Falls turnoff with dangerous, narrow area miles 74 to 81, use only established turnouts for parking the crew vehicle	73.3	2,500
3000’ elevation sign on left	75.8	3,000
3rd Marathon	78.6	3,400
4000’ elevation sign on left	80.2	4,000
Father Crowley’s Point on right	80.2	4,000
Death Valley National Park Boundary	84.9	4,200
Saline Valley turnoff on right	86.0	4,800
5000’ elevation sign	87.0	5,000
Darwin turnoff	90.1	5,050
5000’ elevation sign on left	92.4	5,000
Grave Site on right	96.3	4,100
27.5 mile post marker	100.0	4,050
4000’ elevation sign on left	101.6	4,000
Hwy 136 & 190 go straight	102.9	3,935
4th Marathon	104.8	3,800
Keeler	107.8	3,610
Adopt-a-Highway sign on right	108.5	3,605
Dolomite loop turnoff on right	112.6	3,600
Dolomite loop turnoff on right	116.9	3,610
Owen’s River	117.7	3,610
Hwy 190 & 395 go right	120.3	3,695
Dow Villa Hotel	122.3	3,610
Portal Road traffic light go left	122.4	3,610
Tuttle Creek turnoff on left	122.9	3,770
LA Aqueduct	123.0	3,855
Lone Pine Creek	124.1	4,200
Movie Flat Road on right	125.1	4,590
Lone Pine Creek	125.3	4,800
Horseshoe Meadow on left	125.5	5,000
Cuffe Ranch turnoff on right	126.7	5,100
Olivas Ranch turnoff on left	128.0	5,300
Lone Pine Campground on left with dangerous, narrow area miles 129 –135, use only established turnouts for parking the crew vehicle	129.0	5,700
Lone Pine Creek	129.2	6,000

Location	Mile	Elevation in Feet
Inyo Nat. Forest sign on right	129.5	6,400
Large pullout on right	130.8	6,890
5th Marathon	131.0	7,000
Switchback to left	131.7	7,215
Vista Point	132.4	7,400
"Campsites 39-44" sign on right	133.3	7,700
Meysan Lakes trailhead on left	133.5	8,035
Family Campsites	133.7	8,100
Mt Whitney Portal overflow parking	134.3	8,200
Finish	135	8,360
Mt Whitney Summit	146	14,495

Figure 1 — Death Valley Ultra Course Map

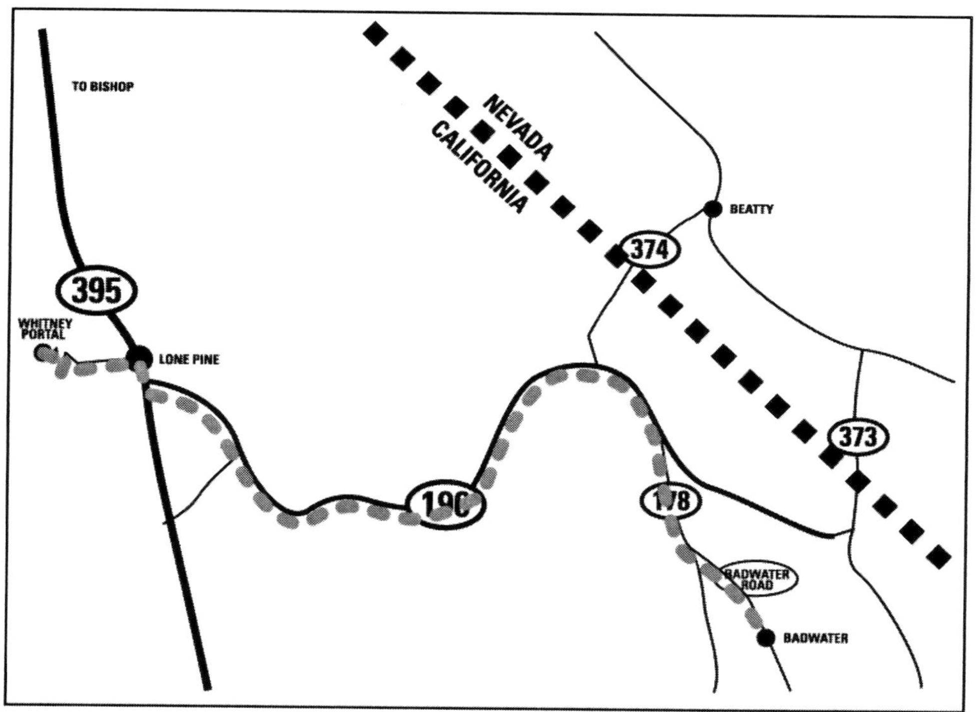

1.3 About The Death Valley Ultra Course

An understanding of the development of Death Valley ultras helps runners and crews appreciate their place in Death Valley and the athletic challenges it allows. Here is a brief summary of the history of ultrarunning in Death Valley.

After about 20 solo efforts had occurred in Death Valley, Hi Tec Sports, USA developed a Badwater 146 running shoe they wanted to promote. In 1987 Brit Adrian Crane and American Tom Possert were engaged by Hi Tec Sports to compete against each other in an endeavor to advertise this shoe. The shoe delaminated in the heat of the competition but the runners went on to the finish and this was the beginning of competition outside of the solo realm. There was no “race” in 1988 but in 1989 the race grew including the Twin Team of Barbara Alvarez and Angelika Castenada along with the concept of crewing. The next year’s invitation included Bill Miller, Carol Carter, and others and front-runners Marshall Ulrich, Tom Possert, Joe Marchand, Odin Christensen, and Jack Christian. Mid-pack and back-of-the-pack runners walked the race after the first marathon and were able to finish with support of their crews. The popularity of the Hi Tec race grew as runners from around the world were intrigued with the challenge of the event and the emerging sport of adventure racing.

Adventure athletes began thinking of innovative and difficult things to do in Death Valley such as crossing from one boundary to another or going cross-country. Then there were the multiple-crossings and solo, self-contained efforts in combination with or separate from the progressive development of official Death Valley ultras. All of these are worth separate stories or books.

To understand the runner’s goal for the Death Valley ultra and to knowledgably accept the responsibilities, crew members need to understand the Death Valley ultra course. Without specific knowledge of Death Valley and the 50 miles after Death Valley up to the Portals of Mt Whitney, it is common to assume that the course is in a valley. As shown in the profile of the course in Figure 2 and the description, the course is not along the bottom of a valley.

Significant Points On The Course

Badwater - Death Valley ultras begin on the pavement near the Badwater pool of saltwater located at the lowest place in the western hemisphere, 282’ below sea level.

Furnace Creek Ranch, Mile 17.4 is the first oasis in a Death Valley ultra with a gas station, small general store, motel, and swimming pool, campsites, and ice machine.

Stove Pipe Wells, Mile 41.9 has a small market, gas station, restaurant, and motel.

Townes Pass (4,956’), Mile 58.7 is ~ a 16-mile long ascent, then a 9-mile descent, followed by several flat miles. Here the Death Valley ultra course is a steep and narrow road with limited opportunities to park.

Figure 2 — Distances and Locations for Death Valley Ultras

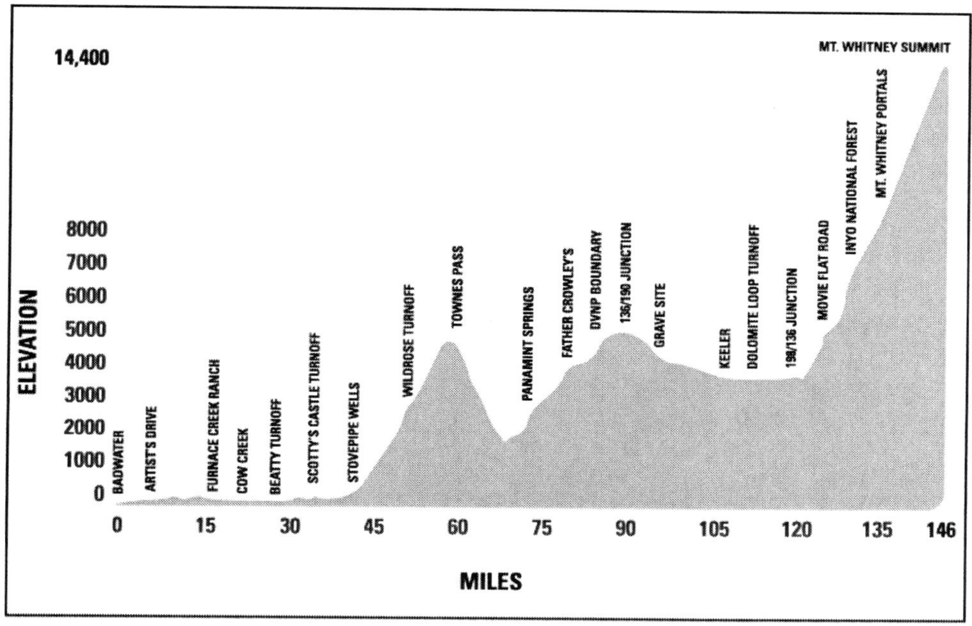

Panamint Springs Resort, Mile 72.3 has a restaurant and motel and gasoline with limited hours. It is the beginning of a long, steep climb on the steep and narrow road with limited opportunities to park.

Father Crowley's Turnout, Mile 80.2 is a wide and welcome parking area but the road continues to rise to 5,000' over rolling hills to the summit near the Darwin Turnoff, then descends into Owen's Valley.

Keeler, Mile 107.8 is a small mining town with no facilities.

Lone Pine, Whitney Portal Road, Mile 122.2 is the first and only town on the Death Valley ultra course and offers fast food, pizza, restaurants, motels, gas stations, grocery stores, etc. Re-supply here for the final segment of the ultra, the climb to the portals, the longest and steepest climb of the race. Temperatures decrease as the elevation rises. Parking pullouts are limited on this winding road.

Mt Whitney Portal, (8,360'), Mile 135 is the finish of official Death Valley ultra races. To celebrate an ultra finish and to prepare for summiting there is a small diner/shop open during daylight hours and a campground.

Mt Whitney Summit, (14,495'), Mile 146 is the highest point in the continental United States.

1.4 What Is In The Guide

The crewing information is organized in practical, useable, discrete topics in the way runners and crew would use the information. The crewing topics are organized in the following chapters:

- Chapter 2 Selecting and Structuring the Crew
- Chapter 3 Scheduling the Crew
- Chapter 4 Selecting Crew Vehicles
- Chapter 5 Pre-event Crewing
- Chapter 6 Crewing During the Event
- Chapter 7 Foot Care
- Chapter 8 Re-supplying
- Chapter 9 Recording the Event
- Chapter 10 Using Pacers
- Chapter 11 Cleaning Up After the Event
- Chapter 12 Crewing For Mt Whitney
- Appendix A Conversions
- Appendix B Humorous Writings of Ben Jones
- Appendix C Death Valley Ultra Pace Chart
- Bibliography

With this information, Death Valley ultra crews can avoid the top 10 Death Valley Ultra Crewing Mistakes.

Top 10 Death Valley Ultra Crewing Mistakes

10. Locking the van keys in the running, closed van while crewing on the ultra course.

9. Running out of gas while crewing on the ultra course.

8. Missing/loosing/not being prepared for the runner on the ultra course.

7. Selecting an open bed truck as a crew vehicle.

6. Attempting to crew out of the trunk of a sedan.

5. Using plastic grocery bags as containers for food items in the crew vehicle.

4. Bringing a crew member to Death Valley who thinks s/he is going on vacation.

3. Loosing an item required for crewing in a messy disorganized van.

2. Falling asleep while crewing.

and the

1 Mistake. Selecting crew members who thinks their condition and feelings take precedence over the runner's.

"We treat more crews for dehydration than runners . . ."

Dr. Lisa Bliss,

2005 Badwater Ultramarathon Medical Director and Badwater Finisher

Chapter 2 — Selecting And Structuring The Crew

Crewing a Death Valley ultra is not for everyone and everyone does not have the characteristics to be a successful crew member for a Death Valley ultra. The runner selecting his/her crew needs to understand the characteristics that make a good crew member and select crew members to make his/her crew team successful to make his/her Death Valley ultra successful. The runner is the team leader as s/he is selecting the crew but when the crew chief is selected, and identified, the crew chief becomes responsible for co-planning much of the ultra with the runner. The crew chief is the decision maker in consultation with the runner before the ultra and the sole decision maker during the ultra. The most successful crew chief consults with crew members for their important input before and during the ultra.

There is the optimum number of crew for a Death Valley ultra.

This chapter provides information and considerations for selecting, structuring, practicing with, and compensating a Death Valley ultra crew. Crew selection is generally done well in advance of the ultra; usually when the runner applies for entry into an official Death Valley ultra event. Ideally the runner identifies crew at the time s/he submits an event application to know that s/he will have the crew support needed if entry to the event is accepted. When the runner is notified of acceptance, the runner can begin discussions with the people s/he identified as meeting the characteristics of successful crew and verify if her/his assessment of the crew candidates characteristics is true and if the logistical plans for schedule, travel, commitment, expenses can be arranged.

Decide about using pacers in a Death Valley ultra when selecting crew since it is efficient from a logistical and a financial standpoint when the same person can function as a crew and pacer.

2.1 Selecting The Crew

The Death Valley ultra runner usually selects his/her crew from friends, family, acquaintances, and ultrarunners who are interested in a Death Valley ultra experience. In selecting the crew, a balance of emotion and practicality produces the most successful crew members. Crew candidates need knowledge about crewing duties and responsibilities, an informed understanding of a Death Valley ultra and the runner's goal for the event, real willingness and ability to be a team member to achieve the runner's goal, and to realize the importance that good health and fitness plays in crewing an endurance desert event.

It is easy for friends, family, and acquaintances to enthusiastically volunteer to be crew and they volunteer to crew a Death Valley ultra for many reasons:

- Interest in the event and/or desert endurance sport
- Concern for the runner's well being at the event
- Desire to experience the event before s/he commits to running a Death Valley ultra
- Commitment to support the runner's racing goal
- Desire for their own adventure
- Repaying the runner a sports favor
- Reciprocating crewing support they received from the runner
- Has time and resources to participate
- Has experience crewing other ultra events

These are good reasons for people to volunteer as crew for a Death Valley ultra but alone, they are not sufficient to select the volunteer crew. Consider people with the following characteristics when selecting crew for a Death Valley ultra:

- Reliable and consistent but flexible
- Good reasoning and critical thinking in unplanned situations
- Healthy, fit, heat trained, and can manage fatigue
- Previous crewing experience
- Experienced in desert environments
- Familiarity with the demands of endurance sport
- Understanding of sports goals
- Understanding and appreciation of the Death Valley environment
- Commitment to the runner's specific Death Valley ultra goals
- Knowledgeable about Death Valley ultras—the course, the history, performances, participants and understanding the format of crewing the runner every mile
- Knowledgeable about Mt Whitney

- Good organization and multitasking ability
- Good care givers
- Good team player

2.2 Structuring The Crew

Structuring a successful Death Valley ultra crew is a challenging, time-consuming planning task. Crew candidates can be scattered throughout time zones and difficult to communicate with as they are involved in their own busy schedules. They are not as consumed with the runner's Death Valley ultra goal as the runner who is training and planning for the Death Valley ultra. Considering these realities, this section provides guidelines about sizing your crew and selecting crew members.

2.2.1 Crew Size

Three is the optimal number of crew for efficiency and small ultra teams better preserve and maintain the character of the unique Death Valley environment. Brining in and managing large crews contradicts the tradition of running in the solitary, remote, extreme environment that is Death Valley. Large crews require resources to support, move, and coordinate through Death Valley. Logistics of large crews can take a higher percentage of effort than the purpose they are there to accomplish--to crew the runner's successful Death Valley ultra.

More than three crew members impact the Death Valley ultra team with diminishing returns from a cost, effort, and safety standpoint.

Certainly there are larger successful crews that support Death Valley ultras, usually associated with front runners' races. Large crews can be successful but this guide focuses on the success of the optimal number of three crew members.

Another consideration of about the number of crew members is the practicality of getting crew members to Death Valley for the ultra event. Because Death Valley is a remote location, difficult and expensive to get to, the fewer crew members whose travel and other logistics must be planned the fewer variables in a complex logistical plan, and the fewer opportunities for problems to occur.

2.2.2 Crew Characteristics and Roles

All crew members can share in the pre-event crewing responsibilities under the direction of t the crew chief and individual crew members will perform aspects of all of the following functions, but select crew members who have the skills or knowledge to accomplish the functions described in Table 2. Inform crew candidates the reasons they are selected and the functions they are expected to perform. If the candidate crew member disagrees with your evaluation of their character or skills, it is important to know before they are expected to perform the function for the crew in Death Valley.

Table 2 — Crew Member Roles

Roles	Responsibilities	Characteristics
Crew Chief	• Plan technical aspects such as pre-event set-up of vehicles, scheduling, managing the logistics of fueling vehicles, re-supplying ice and water, managing the effects of weather, moving vehicles, etc • Understand the course distances, landmarks, official race event, Mt Whitney, etc • Make decisions for the runner and crew to manage circumstances that arise for the runner during the ultra • Know all hotel and vehicle reservations • Be responsible for Mt Whitney permits • Record ultra notes • Delegate responsibilities as appropriate	• Quick thinking • Decision maker • Sense of location/direction • Knowledgeable about endurance sport • Knowledgeable about desert and high altitude environments • Knowledgeable about Death Valley • Knowledge about the official Death Valley race event • Understand the runner's goal and motivation
"Medic"	• Administer foot care, treat blisters, and high-altitude affects • Understand, monitor, and administer hydration, calories, and electrolytes in desert and high altitude environments • Understand, monitor, and administer stomach meds, pain relief meds, any prescription meds to the runner • Make decisions about the runner's health and physical status	• Experience in or understanding of sport medicine in endurance sports • Experience in or understanding of endurance sport in desert and high-altitude environments including foot care altitude sickness • Understand metabolizing hydration and electrolytes in endurance sport in desert and high-altitude environments • Understand the runner's goal and motivation
Psychological Support	• Provide runner-specific psychological support/coaching/motivation during the lower periods of the runner's event	• Runner's family member, spouse, loved one, close friend • Understand the psychology of endurance sport • Understand the runner's goal and motivation
Driver/ "Engineer"	• Drive the crew vehicle during the Death Valley ultra • Perform auto mechanic service on the crew vehicles and other gear	• Good driving skills with larger loaded vehicles • Good auto mechanic skills and general ability with how things work to fix broken gear or engineer a solution quickly
"Accountant"	• Calculate remaining gas in the crew and shuttle vehicles and time based on the runner's pace distances to next gas stations • Track ice and water requirements and time based on the runner's pace and distances to next re-supply	• Aptitude with distance, pace, measurement, and relationships to time • Act as treasurer for the team, keeping the team's money or credit cards for fuel, supplies, etc • Collect receipts associated with expenses for the event

Roles	Responsibilities	Characteristics
	• Calculate runner's pace and projected time to various checkpoints, rest stops, etc • For international teams: • Convert US units of measure (gallons, ounces, Fahrenheit, etc) to metric units • Convert U.S dollars to foreign currency	• Tally total expense reimbursements due crew members
"Publicist"	• Handle requests for contact with the runner from the media • Photograph &/or video the runner's event • Function as the media contact for the runner and manage media access to the runner	• Instinct to know when the runner can communicate have contact with the media without affecting the race • Persuasive personality to positively present the runner's race to the media when it is not an appropriate time for the media to have contact the runner • Distribute press releases on the runner's race to local media before the event and when the event is complete

2.3 Practicing With The Crew

There is a value and advantage to train in the desert especially with the crew members in preparation for a Death Valley ultra. Training in Death Valley and on Mt Whitney grew in popularity in the early 1990s. Modeled after the training camps Norm Klein, the Race Director for the Western States 100 Endurance Run held over 3 days several weeks prior to that event, "Badwater" Ben Jones held the first Heat Training Clinic in the mid-1990s hosting Bill Menard and crew. Bill went on to win the race.

Traditionally the no-fee clinics were held on Memorial Day weekend (end of May) and Fourth of July weekends starting at Stovepipe Wells Village and covering up to 65 miles over the 3 days. These organized sessions to train in the heat include seminars regarding blister/foot care, heat-related-illness awareness, and group treks.

Since the beginning of the clinics groups of over 40 participants, primarily runners training for official Death Valley ultra races and their crews, assembled for the clinics. The clinics where runners and crew become oriented to the Death Valley ultra venue and crewing situations produced a race finish rate for about 85% of the attendees and there were fewer problems for the crew members. This rate demonstrates the value of practicing in the Death Valley environment simulating conditions of an ultrarun and learning crewing techniques.

Since 2000 liability issues have arisen due to the numbers of people involved in formal Death Valley ultras. High participation has stretched the Death Valley National Park staff as well as their rescue service personnel and an ambulance is required for safety for the organized-for-profit events. With this requirement, the smaller, solo efforts are easier and safer. Practice sessions can take place just outside of Park such as in the lower half of Panamint Valley, a location that mimics Death Valley National Park terrain.

Practice high-altitude trail running with the team to prepare for summiting Mt Whitney. During this training use the mountain gear the team will use on Mt Whitney such as the water filtration pump, poles, daypacks with bladders, etc to ensure you know how to use it. It doesn't take long to realize an inexpensive low-volume water filtration pump takes too much time and effort to fill each team member's 70-ounce bladder.

2.4 Compensating The Crew

While the time and effort that a crew member offers a Death Valley ultra runner is priceless, the cost to crew is able to be calculated. There are reasons to compensate crew and reasons to not compensate crew. The reasons a runner may not compensate crew include the following.

- A crew member can be repaying a Death Valley ultra runner for crewing him/her in a previous ultra event.
- A crew member is a family member who is crewing for love, not money.
- A crew member may be investing in the experience of learning to crew an ultra in Death Valley or accumulating a desert ultra experience to enhance his/her sports resume.
- A crew member appreciates the unique Death Valley environment and is eager to spend time there under any circumstance.

There are practical reasons to compensate all crew that include the following:

- A crew candidate may not be able to crew without financial support; s/he may not have financial resources to cover the cost of crewing.
- For employed crew members, they may be taking time off work and loosing income to crew for a week in Death Valley.
- Death Valley is a remote location to travel to and getting there can be an expense for crew members.
- Money is an incentive for humans and being "paid" can be a factor for a crew member to perform beyond fatigue and level of comfort.
- Crewing is hard, demanding work that not everyone can do.
- You get what you pay for and when crew members are "free," their commitment and ability may reflect that price.

- Compensating crew for their time, effort, and expense recognizes those contributions and shows appreciation for what they are giving to the success of the runner's ultra.

Although there is no standard monetary value associated with crewing, when a runner plans to compensate crew, the following items relate to Death Valley ultra crew member's expenses and can be considered in the compensation calculation:

- Travel expenses — air, ground transportation, rental vehicle
- Loss of income from not working for employed crew members
- Lodging expenses
- Communications expenses — long distance calls to plan the ultra and calls from Death Valley
- Incidentals purchased on the ultra course

When a runner is compensating a crew member(s), the runner should clearly identify how s/he will make the compensation. The compensation plan should address all aspects of the compensation including when and how the compensation is to be made. For example, for crew compensation involving air fares, identify who makes air travel reservations, when the reservation is to be made, travel times, departure/arrival locations, and how and when the air fares will be paid.

The most important thing is a good crew that has an ultra background.

-- Mark Godale, Badwater Ultramarathon Second Place Finisher 1999

Chapter 3 — Scheduling The Crew

Schedule crews in 12-hour "working" and 12-hour "resting" shifts where two crew members are working at all times. Yes, this schedule requires that one crew member is crewing for a 24-hour period, which is humanly possible. After all, running a Death Valley ultra is a huge effort on the runner's part and it is not unrealistic to expect crew to extend themselves in support of the runner's effort.

When transitioning between rested and active crew members, allow time to update the runners status.

Consider the following circumstances when scheduling crew shifts.

- All crew members generally go to the start in one vehicleand are at the finish so the entire team is together for those periods.
- Realize that the daytime working shifts are generally more frenetic than night-time working shifts because of the efforts to manage the runner during the most dangerous temperatures. Also, the beginning of the event when runner and crew are most fresh and enthusiastic generally is in the morning.
- Calculate travel time from the runner and back to the runner on the course in scheduling the resting shift period.
- Provide specific instructions about any tasks the resting crew member needs to accomplish during his/her resting shift such as re-supplying food items or ice, checking out of a hotel, making phone calls, picking up Mt Whitney permits form the Forest Service Office, etc.
- Use the small, support car to drive resting crew members to and from hotel rest sites.
- Identify crew members' driving preferences such as poor night driving vision, experience with driving winding mountain roads, experience driving a fully packed van, etc to schedule crew members' driving preferences with shifts on the various sections of the course.
- Allow time to brief and debrief crew transitioning between on and off shifts. The departing crew must inform the arriving crew of status of the runner over the previous 12 hours, what is planned for the next crew

stop, and any unusual, unplanned events. Depending on how busy the time of transition is with crewing activities, the transition may take several crew stops.

- As early as possible make reservations for hotel rooms along the course for crew to rest to ensure the crew has accommodations to rest during the event. The Death Valley ultra window of July and August is tourist season in Death Valley and many tourists are staying at Death Valley hotels during this time.

Lodging Reservation Information for Death Valley Ultras

The Furnace Creek Inn
CA Hwy.190
760.786.2361
http://www.furnacecreekresort.com
66 rooms
Elegant 4 diamond resort in an oasis

Stovepipe Wells Village
CA Hwy.190 (west park)
760.786.2387
http://www.stovepipewells.com
83 rooms
Ranch style village; uncomplicated atmosphere, a 10-minute walk to Sand Dunes

Dow Villa Motel
310 South Main Street
Lone Pine, California 93545
800.824.9317 760 876-5521
dowvilla@lonepinetv.com
http://www.dowvillamotel.com/
AAA three-diamond rated motel

The Furnace Creek Ranch
CA Hwy.190
800.528.6367 760.786.2345
http://www.furnacecreekresort.com
224 rooms
19th century historic ranch

Panamint Springs Resort
Hwy.190 West end of Death Valley National Park
775.482.7680 760.764.2002 x234
http://www.deathvalley.com
Small western-style resort located in the Panamint Valley in Death Valley National Park

These resources are correct as of printing but may change or may not be available due to other circumstances.

This chapter describes the activities of the resting Death Valley ultra crew and crewing the night shift.

3.1 Resting Crew Activities

When a crew member starts his/her resting shift it is not the same as getting off work from a long shift as a laborer. Although 12 hours seems like a long time, it can go by very fast unless the resting crew member remains focused on the resting goal. Returning fresh, alert, rested, and strong to the crew is the goal of a resting shift. Here are considerations for a successful resting shift.

- When departing the crew vehicle:
  - Obtain a written list of tasks from the crew chief that you must accomplish while you are away from the crew vehicle. Such tasks include fueling the shuttle vehicle, buying specified amounts of ice, water, food, or other supplies, checking into and/or out of a hotel, picking up permits for Mt Whitney, making calls, disposing of trash from the crew vehicle, etc.
  - Ensure that the resting crew member has the hotel reservation number and know whose name the reservation was made. If the hotel room is already in your team's control, ensure that you have the key for the room.
  - Understand what time the resting crew member is to return and where the runner and crew are expected to be on the course at that projected return time.
  - Check that the resting crew member is not taking any item such as back up crew vehicle keys, overflow supplies from the crew vehicle, lighting not used in the day time, etc in the shuttle car.
  - Verify that the resting crew member is taking his/her gear from the crew van.
- When the resting crew member travels to the hotel destination to rest, avoid the temptation to visit with friends who may be on the ultra course. It is interesting to see friends on the course but they are working and should not be distracted from their priority. Greet or cheer the runners and crew but don't stop to visit. Visiting diminishes the time you have to accomplish your resting crew activities and to rest.
- Consult the written list and procure items that the resting crew member is requested to procure.
- Save all receipts for items purchased.
- When the resting crew member arrives at the hotel, check in immediately to confirm that the reservation is available. Limited resources during large Death Valley ultras can impact reservations availability.
- Prioritize the rest by cooling off in a swimming pool, showering, sleeping, and eating. Now is not the time for site seeing, shopping, etc.

- Set an alarm clock and allow adequate time to return to and search for your runner and crew on the course especially in the dark.
- When returning to the crew van, look for the runner, crew vehicle, or runner's stake out marker. It can be difficult to find these items in the night when there are other runners and vehicles surrounding your runner.

3.2 Crewing The Night Shift

Crewing a Death Valley ultra at night is a wonderful experience. A priceless bonus of a Death Valley ultra is the night sky: the stars in the Death Valley sky are spectacular and a lifetime memory. Surprisingly the temperatures that drop 30 some degrees from the 120s into the 90s, can feel "cold" after a day working in the desert temperatures and sun. At the higher altitudes on the course, temperatures can feel cold. Here are considerations about crewing a Death Valley ultra at night.

- To transition the runner and pacer to night gear start preparing the night gear — reflective vest, blinking light, head lamp or hand held flashlight — before it gets dark. At night the runner no longer needs to protect his/her head from the sun with a hat or wear sun-protection clothing.
- The van needs to be transitioned to night time crewing as well. To assist the runner and pacer in finding the van among other vans in the proximity as can occur in an official ultra race, secure a distinctive colorful or blinking light on the rear of the van in a location that can been seen by the approaching runner and pacer when the van's back door is open.
- Nigh is cooler than the day so the crew isn't as busy as they were in the day. The runner doesn't require as much cooling and does not have to wear as much sun-protection clothing. Also, the runner's pace can slow at night although the cooler temperatures and the relief from the sun's heat can be reinvigorating for runners who had to slow the pace in the heat of the day. Often it is easier to process fluid and calories during the "cool" night.
- Because night is the natural cycle for sleep and it is quieter and more peaceful after a frantic day of crewing, crew can feel sleepy enclosed by darkness. Stimulants such as caffeine in the form of instant coffee made with "room temperature" water, soda, or caffeine pills can be helpful.
- Runners who do not ordinarily use or want pacers may use a pacer to help keep him/her awake during the night. The pacer must wear the same

night gear as the runner but the pacer's light is sufficient to warn on coming traffic of the runner and pacer on the road and to light the way for both the runner and the pacer. With the pacer carrying the lighting the runner saves that energy. The runner and the pacer both require crewing, increasing the work of the crew.

- While there are no bugs bothering the runner and crew during the day, they come out with a vengeance at night drawn to the light in the van. Using headlamps for lighting instead of the interior lights in the van reduce the bugs attracted to lights in van.

> *"We alternate crews so each one could theoretically get 6 hours of sleep."*
>
> *Don Meyer, 2001, Badwater Ultramarathon finisher and 2000, 2002, 2003, 2004, and 2005 crew*

Scheduling The Crew

Chapter 4 — Selecting Crew Vehicles

This chapter describes considerations for selecting crew vehicles to use for the most optimal crewing experience at a Death Valley ultra and information about how to rent them. Crew vehicles can greatly impact the crewing experience and the success of the runner's event. Vehicles in the stress of the Death Valley environment break down more readily than in a normal use environment. Operating for up to 60 hours non-stop in average temps of 110 degrees requires a reliable and good performing vehicle.

4.1 Choosing Crew Vehicles

When selecting crew vehicles for a Death Valley ultra, consider the following:

- The balance of performance with limited access to gasoline
- Compliance with official race requirements on size requirements
- Maneuverability and stability on the winding, narrow sections of the Death Valley ultra road
- Traction on the soft shoulders of the Death Valley ultra road
- Reputation of the manufacturer's air conditioning

For the optimal crew of three, select vehicles from the following two categories:

- The crew minivan, not a cargo or full-size van
- A small shuttle/commuter car to run errands and to drive the resting crew from the course to the hotel and back and store crew gear, mountain gear, and supplies that are not needed for immediate use in the crew van

Do not use the following vehicles as a crew vehicle:

- A recreational vehicle of any type; an RV may serve as a base station but is not suited for crew stops every 1-mile
- A pick up truck with a covered or open bed
- A sedan

Consider the following features in selecting the crew van.

- Compliance with official event rules for vehicle width and type and where certain vehicle types are permitted/prohibited on the event course
- White or metallic (gold and silver) exterior and a light color interior
- Makes of vehicles that have better performing air conditioning

- For the van, two rows of removable or foldable/retractable passenger seats
- A place to store the removed middle row of passenger seats during the event if the crew van is a rental picked up at an airport in route to the ultra
- Sliding doors on both sides of the van for easy access
- A rear door that opens upward but that can be easily reached and closed by shorter and less strong members of the crew
- A driver's seat that can be adjusted for all members of the crew
- Highway assistance programs available for the van
- Marking the exterior of the van with the runner name and number with a material that is removable and does not damage the vehicle

4.2 Renting Crew Vehicles

After you understand the types of vehicles you need to crew a Death Valley ultra, decide if you have access to such vehicles and if it is practical to drive the vehicles to Death Valley. If the team does not have access to crew vehicles and/or if it is not practical to get vehicles to Death Valley, the vehicles will need to be rented from a car rental company.

If the runner and crew are flying to Death Valley, generally the airport that you are flying to is the practical location to rent the vehicles. For runners and crew coming from locations close enough to Death Valley to make driving gear and crew members practical from a time and economic standpoint, vehicles could be rented from car rental companies near their home locations.

When renting vehicles for use in Death Valley, limit the information you offer the rental company about the use of the vehicle. Generally a statement about touring, sight seeing, vacationing is sufficient explanation of the purpose as is stating that the destination is California or "the desert".

Ensure that all crew members who will drive the crew vehicles are present with their license when the rental vehicles are picked up. Secure insurance and roadside service for rentals to be used in a Death Valley ultra. Death Valley is a long way from civilization and it can be hours before non-emergency help can arrive.

Once the crew gets organized, there might be a few extra minutes here and here to spare, but not enough to be reading a book or anything.

Mike Henebry, author of "Running Badwater"

Chapter 5 — Pre-event Crewing

Do not store unnecessary crew gear, runner items not used for the race, or mountain gear in the van.

The pre-event crew responsibilities in Death Valley are substantial and demanding even if the temperature isn't 115 degrees when the pre-event crew tasks are performed. This chapter describes these tasks in the following sections:

- 5.1 Pre-event Crewing Responsibilities
- 5.2 Organizing The Van
- 5.3 Organizing the Crew Shuttle Vehicle

To convert the units of measure mentioned for any of the gear or volumes discussed in this guide, Appendix A includes information on conversion of metric and U.S. units.

5.1 Pre-event Crewing Responsibilities

Pre-event crewing responsibilities are numerous and include the individualized tasks of getting all crew members, the runner, and the team's gear to Death Valley from locations around the world. After that logistical challenge is accomplished the specific pre-event crewing responsibilities begin. Here is a list of pre-event crewing responsibilities that successful runners and crews must accomplish before the Death Valley ultra.

Before Arriving In Death Valley

- Prepare the runner's pace chart to calculate projected time at various milestones on the Death Valley ultra course. Select significant milestones from Table 1 and enter the runner's projected time to the milestone in the runner calculator at http://www.csgnetwork.com/runnerscalc.html or a similar calculator to calculate the pace required to reach the milestone. Verify this pace against the runner's fitness, health, training, heat training, course geography to the milestone to ensure the pace is realistic. Realize that a continuous 20-minute mile pace coves the 135-mile course from the Badwater pond to Whitney Portals in a good finish time of 45 hours. Also realize that a continuous 20-minutes/mile pace with crewing and foot care stops may not be as easy as it sounds. Record all of these projected times to milestones on the runner's pace chart, distribute it to the crew, and take it to the Death Valley ultra.

To determine the pace the runner needs to run to achieve a specific time goal or to determine the time a pace will produce, consult the Death Valley Ultra Pace Chart in Appendix C. This chart identifies pace requirements over the last 35 miles of the Death Valley ultra course.

- Treat feet over time to get calluses thin with pedicure file because the conditions presented by a Death Valley ultra cause more extensive problems than usual when feet blister. Thickened skin that is of value under normal ultrarunning conditions, produces blisters that are difficult to fix and are painful. The friction from the paved, canted road and the heat prevail over the protection of the callus and blisters develop deep under the callus. If a callus is thick and a blister develops in the callus area, it is impossible to drain and it grows in size and pain as miles add up. Trim toenails square and file them so no rough edges remain. Realize that there are only a few runners who finish a Death Valley ultra without some form of foot taping to fix blisters. It is the taping that enables them to finish.
- Make arrangements to rent a satellite phone for use in Death Valley for emergency situations. Locate a satellite phone rental resource by conducting an internet search for satellite phone rental.
- Read and understand all published official race rules.
- Obtain a permit for the Mt Whitney trail through the Inyo National Forest Mt Whitney Ranger District, PO Box 8, Lone Pine, CA 93545, 760-876-6200. Permits are limited and should be requested in February through a lottery for the best chance of getting them for the day for the day after the ultra when the climb is scheduled. The cost for the permit is nominal. For permit information go to http://www.fs.fed.us/r5/inyo/recreation/wild/permitsres.shtml.
- Make reservations for hotels in Death Valley for the day(s) before the event, during the event, and after.

Foods that Work Better in Crewing a Death Valley Ultra:

- Choose tortillas over a loaf of bread for sandwiches. A loaf of bread is easy to squish in the active crew van and a slice of bread dries into toast when it is exposed to the desert air.
- Choose potatoes chips in cans instead of bags.
- Choose items that come in secure protective containers or that can be repackaged into secure, protective containers.
- Avoid items that can leak, melt, puncture, or ooze.

Pre-event Crewing

See the **Lodging Reservation Information for Death Valley Ultras** in Chapter 3.

- Prepare a contact list of the runner and all crew members with the following information and distribute it to the team:
    - Legal name
    - Mailing address
    - Phone numbers
    - Emergency contact information
    - Medical/health conditions that are affected by desert endurance or mountaineering circumstances
- Prepare a media list of media contacts interested in your Death Valley ultra if you want media coverage. Contact these media about you Death Valley ultra training and schedule. Take this media contact list to Death Valley to update them about your finish.
- Plan the amount of supplies the runner and crew needs based on the amount of time the runner estimates s/he will be on the ultra course. If a situation arises during the ultra to extend this time, the supplies will be effected and possible the re-supply schedule. Here are the major supplies to plan.
    - For water, calculate the amount needed based the on approximately 15 ounce per crew member and runner per hour for the total estimated hours of the ultra. This water calculation covers drinking and spraying needs and is more of a total <u>fluid</u> calculation. Neither the runner nor the crew is going to drink exclusively water. Other fluids that the team consumes such as soda, electrolyte drinks, bottled coffee/teas, etc can be considered part of this general calculation. Also, the ice melting in the drinking cooler produces drinking water. And ice melting in the refrigerator cooler produces water for spraying, and soaking towels, chamois, etc. For a team of three crew member with a crew person resting during the middle of the ultra and runner with a projected finish time of 2 days this is approximately 23 gallons of water.

15 oz water x 3.5 people = 52.5 oz/hr x 48 hr = 25,200 oz ÷ 128 oz = 20 gal

- The amount of ice needed is based on the coolers used. Based on the cooler use and configuration recommended in Table 4, a total of 4 blocks of ice and 12 bags of ice cubes are required to fill the coolers.

- For the runner's food, the runner's calorie requirement is based on his/her experience as an ultra runner over the projected time of the ultra. It is human nature to be optimistic in planning the optimal circumstances for nutrition and calories that the runner will consume in the Death Valley ultra. Likely the optimistic planning will not be the reality so plan alternative and additional nutrition for the runner.
- For crew food, calculate food at a slight increased over a regular day's worth of calories for crew to cover the energy expended to crew.
- Calculate pacer calories based on the pacer's experience as a runner running the distance s/he is scheduled to pace in addition to the pacer's calorie requirements for a regular day of nutrition when s/he is not pacing.
- Increase all food estimates by 10% to cover circumstances that keep the runner on the ultra course longer than projected.
- Gasoline is limited to the locations and times listed in Table 8. Because circumstance can change quickly requiring the runner to be on the course longer than projected, the plan for gasoline supply is to always fill the crew van tank when there is an opportunity.

- Practice foot care and taping described in Chapter 7.
- Acclimate to heat and altitude. See guidelines for heat acclimation in Section 6.3.2.1 and for altitude acclimation in Section 12.2.
- For use on Mt Whitney, purchase a high volume water filter that can remove bacteria, virus, and metals that is as light as the features allow. Practice using the water filter. Filtering water for three 70-ounce bladders and three 20-ounce water bottles can be a tedious task. Invest in a quality water filtration pump with efficiency, volume, and health/safety features.
- For teams traveling to Death Valley in a personal van from home, collect gear listed in Table 3. For teams flying to Death Valley, develop a plan to transport or to buy large gear such as coolers. If you are taking coolers on a plane, pack other gear inside the cooler. If you flying to Death Valley and plan to purchase coolers on the drive into Death Valley, there are some locations with stores. Prepare a thoughtful plan about how you will get your gear to Death Valley.

Pre-event Crewing

The Day Before The Ultra

- Obtain Death Valley National Park permits for each crew vehicle at the park entrance and secure the permit on the dashboards of the vehicles so the permit is visible. There are four entrances into Death Valley but only two locations to pay entrance fees: Furnace Creek Visitor's Center and the swipe card kiosk at Stovepipe Wells for paying with major credit cards. The four entrances to Death Valley are:
  - From the east via Beatty, Nevada
  - On Highway 190 via Death Valley Junction
  - On Highway 190 from the south via Shoshone.
  - From the west via Trona, Olancha, and Lone Pine
- Check into the hotel where you have reservations.
- Attend any official event's mandatory meeting and complete the event's required paperwork.
- Conduct a team pre-race meeting to discuss and plan the following topics:
  - Runner nutrition, hydration, and electrolyte amounts, frequency, and how these are to be given to the runner
  - Runner pace chart that includes times for the key distances and locations in Table 1
  - When/if the runners wants to be informed of his pace/progress/place in a competitive Death Valley ultra
  - Strategies/methods for managing/implementing cooling the runner described in Section 6.3.2.2
  - Strategies/methods for managing/implementing foot care described in Chapter 7, and health issues described in Section 6.3.3
  - Strategies/methods for managing/implementing rest breaks, off-course breaks, emergency breaks described in Section 6.4
  - Strategies/methods for managing re-supplying in Chapter 8 including methods for paying for re-supplies
  - Strategies/methods for managing emotional/motivation issues described in Section 6.6

  - Circumstances that require withdrawing from the ultra as discussed in Section 6.4.4
  - Crew roles and responsibilities described in Chapter 2
  - Crew shifts, schedules, and logistics described in Chapter 3
  - Climbing Mt Whitney described in Chapter 12
  - Cleaning up after the ultra described in Chapter 11
  - Traveling from the Death Valley ultra including departure schedules and locations
  - The importance of team work of the crew to meet the runner's goal
  - The concerns the runner has about the ultra and how to address them

- Purchase ice and arrange it in the coolers as listed in Table 4.
- Organizing crew vehicles as described in Sections 5.2 and 5.3.
- Fuel the vehicles.
- Program the satellite phone with local emergency phone numbers listed in Section 6.4.3.
- Ensure that the runner is well hydrated and feed well through the day.

The Night Before The Ultra

- Prepare the clothing, shoes, medications, nutrition, and hydration the runner will need for the start of the ultra.
- Tape the runner's feet if necessary. See Chapter 7 Foot Care.
- Lightly massage the runner's legs.
- Ensure the runner has the nutrition and hydration needed the night before the event.
- Place all items not needed for the night and the morning of the event in the organized van or shuttle vehicle.

The Morning Of The Ultra

- If the runner's feet were pre-taped, check that any rough edges of the tape are secure.
- Ensure the runner has his/her pre-event nutrition and hydration.

- Check out of the hotel if the hotel stay is complete and move everything out of the hotel room and to the vehicles.
- Ensure the runner has the items necessary to start the event:
  - Bib number for official ultra races
  - Personal sound system if preferred by the runner
  - Water bottle
  - Sun and heat protection
- Take photos of the team at the Badwater pond and at the start line.

5.2 Organizing The Van

There is an enormous amount of gear required for a safe, convenient, healthy, successful Death Valley ultra. Assembling the gear is challenging but the bigger challenge is to get it to Death Valley and the biggest challenge is to organize it in the crew van. The impossible challenge is to keep it organized and able to be found throughout the entire event by all crew members.

What is obvious to find in the brilliant light of day can be difficult to find after it has been used multiple times during the event and you must locate the item in the cramped van in the dark. This section identifies the 100+ items of gear and supplies listed in Table 3 that are used during a Death Valley ultra and ways to organize and arrange them in the crew vehicles.

Table 3 — Death Valley Ultra Gear And Supplies

Items	Use
"Kitchen" Supplies	
Two 15-gallon ice chests with drain	Function as ice storage & "refrigerator" coolers
One 5-gallon cooler with spigot	Contain & cool the water source
One 45-gallon cooler—optional replacement for one 15-gallon ice chests with drain	Prevents the need to re-supply ice on the course but are not widely available and can be difficult to transport to Death Valley
Ice scoop	Scoop ice cubes from the ice cooler for water bottles to prevent contamination of ice by dirty hands
Mallet or ice pick	Break up ice that melts into large, unusable clumps
• Small plastic funnels • Large plastic funnel	• Pour drink powder into water bottles to prevent spilling in the van and blowing away in the wind • Scoop ice from the ice cooler
Plastic tarp	Tape with duct tape to the passenger area of the van to aid in cleanup after the event.
Trash bags	Contain trash
Hand broom	Clean the floor of the van
Box of zip-lock baggies for	Store & separate food, ice for medical needs, sorting and separating gear
Folding knife	Cut food items
10 ea disposable plates, bowls, cups, and utensils	Serve food items

Pre-event Crewing

Items	Use
Role of paper towels	Clean up after preparing food
Container of antiseptic wet wipes	Clean hands before preparing food
Plastic see-through box or open crates that you can stick your fingers though such as egg or milk crates	Contain kitchen supplies
Medical Supplies	
3 towels	Soak with water & apply to the runner's head, neck, shoulders, torso, & legs for cooling
3 sponges	Soak with water & wipe down runner's heated leg muscles
Chamois	Soak with water & apply to the runner's head, neck, shoulders, torso, & legs for cooling
Toilet paper	Personal hygiene for the runner and crew during outdoor bathroom stops
Electrolytes pills or powder	Maintain electrolyte balance for the runner & crew/pacers
Sodium tablets	Use to maintain sodium balance to process fluid through the runner's & pacer's stomachs
Pain management medications	Minimize muscle pain
Caffeine pills or stimulant source	Keep the runner & crew/pacers alert
Sun block, lip balm, zinc oxide, etc	Protect skin from sun burn
Eye moisture drops	Moisten runner's & crew/pacer's dry eyes
Basic first aid kit	Administer to runner's & crew/pacer's first aid needs
Electronic thermometer with ear probes	Monitor body temperature
Antiseptic wet wipes	Clean hands before first aid procedures & after bathroom stops
Anti-chaffing lubricant	Prevent or alleviate chaffing
Runner's prescription medications and supplements	Maintain dose of prescription meds & supplements
Plastic bucket/basin	Wet towels, chamois, & sponges
Plastic see-through box with handle and latch	Contain medical supplies
Tote carrier with handle	Carry all items from the van to crew the runner
Analog scale	Weigh runner to determine hydration and fluid processing and retention
Calories and Hydration	
Multiple 20-oz water bottles with hand straps	Carry hydration & liquid calories when the runner & pacers are on the ultra course
Gallons of bottled water based on 15 to 20 ounces per team member less the amount of water in 0.5 liter bottles	Provide sanitary, source of drinking water to pour from the drinking water cooler into water bottles to mix with powdered calories or electrolyte mixes
Case(s) of 0.5-liter bottled water based on 15 to 20 ounces per team member less the amount of water in gallon jugs	Provide sanitary, small source of water to drink alone or mixed with powdered calories or electrolyte mixes
Sports fluid replacement for runner & crew/pacers	Maintain electrolytes and provide calories for runner and crew/pacers
Liquid carbohydrate source such as Ensure or sports carbohydrate powder	Provide easily digested calories
Food for runner and crew	Maintain calories for runner & crew/pacers
Dehydrated foods such as, cup-of-soup, cup of instant oatmeal, etc	Function as "meals" for breaks that can be reconstituted w/ hot water heated at "room temperature"
Snacks/comfort food	Maintain calories & lift morale for runner & crew/pacers
Open top plastic see-through boxes to	Contain the calories and hydration items not stored in coolers
Runner's Gear	
Multiple pieces of full coverage solar-protective clothing	Provide protection from sun, wind, & sand
Shorts & light shirts made of technical fabric	Wear for night running when temperatures cool

Pre-event Crewing

Items	Use
Under garments that prevent chaffing	Provide comfort
Event number	Identify runner in official Death Valley ultra & comply with official rules
Several light-colored pairs of running shoes including a larger size	Provide foot care/protection in changing circumstances during the ultra
Orthotics or insoles for cushioning & insulation form the heat	Provide foot care/protection in changing circumstances during the ultra
Socks	Protect foot from friction, moisture to minimize blistering
Hats with long-bill or wide brim plus shroud	Provide sun protection
Sunglasses	Protect eyes from sun, glare, wind, & blowing sand
Nose shield that fits on glasses (optional)	Provide sun protection
Goggles	Protect eyes from sun, glare, wind, & blowing sand
Several bandanas	Used to wet with water & roll ice cubes to cool the runner's & pacers necks
Personal toiletries in a cosmetic bag or shaving kit	Personal hygiene
Feminine hygiene products	Feminine hygiene
Eyeglasses or contact lenses and solutions	Help with runner's vision
Personal sound system and recorded sound	Entertain/distract/focus the runner
Sports bag or clear plastic storage	• Contain runner's gear • Easily identifiable as runner's gear • Able to be tied to handles and hanger hooks in the van
Smaller sports bag or mesh bags	Segregate used/soiled runner's gear
Night Gear	
Reflective vest	Make runner & pacer's visible during night running
Small strobe light or flashers	Make runner & pacer's visible & distinguishable during night running
Lighting such as light weight hand-held flashlights and headlamps for runners and crew	Provide lighting for traffic & for crew to see runner & pacer & comply with official race rules
Small blinking light	Make the van distinguishable to approaching runner & pacers during night running
Extra flashlights/headlamps and batteries	Provide back up for failed lighting
Small, battery operated lantern	For lighting crew activities in the van during extended breaks during the night to prevent the use of disturbing interior dome lights while the runner is resting in the van
Open top plastic see-through box or mesh bag takes less room	Contain the night gear
"Office" Supplies	
Clipboard with pen attached with a string	Provide a surface to record Death Valley Notes Template recordings & keep pace chart, note paper, & other event documents secure from blowing away in the wind
Pens & pencils	Use to record information on the Death Valley Notes Template
Permanent marker	Mark zip-lock bags & containers to identify contents
Note paper	Write list for supplies, hotel room numbers, phone numbers, etc for crew who are shuttling to rest activities
• Satellite phones • Cellular phone optional as service is unreliable • Two-way radios with a 2-mile radius	• Contact a local GlobalStar store for satellite phone rental information • Use for communication when service is available • Use to communicate between crew members to reduce running back and forth to crew the runner
Two-way radios to use between the crew vehicles (optional)	Use for pacer to communicate with crew about runner's needs and status

Pre-event Crewing

Items	Use
Crisp $1 bills	Pay for ice from ice vending machine
~$200 USD in cash	Pay for gas, ice, supplies, etc purchased during the event
Credit card	Pay for lodging, gas, ice, supplies, food, etc
Bank deposit-like bag with zipper	Keep money, credit cards, and receipts for supplies bought on the race course
Inyo County, Death Valley, Owens Valley, and Whitney topo maps	Optional but consider National Geographic California Topo series especially for Mt Whitney
Camera and supplies/accessories	Record the event
Print version of official event information	Consult for official rules and event information
Runner's pace chart	Consult to check runner's projected pace against actual pace and to project time for milestones
Death Valley Ultra Notes Template	• Record all aspects of the runner's race mile by mile to track runner's condition, health, nutrition & hydration intake, treatment, meds, output, progress, & the temperature • Consult for information on these items & for planning and re-supply
Mid-size plastic see-through container with lid	Contain office supplies
Hardware	
Spray bottle with wide mouth opening	Use to cool the runner when running
Duct tape bungee cords, rope, cord, string	Use for repairs or maintenance needs that occur
Scissors	Use for repairs or maintenance that occurs
Safety pins	Use for repairs or maintenance that occurs
2 folding lawn/camp chairs	Use for the runner to rest during breaks or foot care treatment
Small tool kit and road flares	Use for auto repairs
Stock of multiple size batteries for all runner and crew equipment	Replace dead batteries in battery powered gear
Small plastic see-through container with lid	Contain hardware items
Mountain Gear For Summiting Mt Whitney	
Mt Whitney permit	Allow legal use to climb Mt Whitney on the hiking trail
Sunglasses, summit goggles &/or shields for side-stems of sunglasses	Protect eyes against side-glare from sun and snow
Headlamps, lightweight flashlights and batteries Batteries loose power in very cold temperatures.	Providing lighting to see the trail in the dark
Photon micro LED light aka, "keychain" light	Small light to use to replace batteries in the dark
Retractable trekking poles	Assist fatigued runners and runners with sore feet in climbing
Trail shoes or light hiking boots and wool blend socks	Provide optimal footing with light shoe construction
Crampons depending on the snow coverage	Assist in climbing when snow covers the trail
Altitude sickness medication such as Altitude Adjustment	• Reduce high-altitude sickness symptoms • Altitude Adjustment available at www.runningdelights.com
Water purification filter	Prevent Giardia from water taken from the Whitney trail to drink during the climb

Pre-event Crewing

Items	Use
Cold temperature/mountaineering clothing such as: • Wind resistant hiking pants with zip off legs that can be worn as shorts or pants • Fleece jacket • Rain/wind jacket • Gortex jacket for precipitation and cold temperatures • Gloves • Hat	Provide protection against cold, wind, and snow
Ball cap to protect head and eyes from sun in warm temperatures	Protect head and eyes against sun
Camelback-type back pack	Carry mountain gear, calories, and fluid for the crew member and runner
Hydration and calories	Provide hydration until replenishing water on the mountain and calories for the entire climb
Camera	Photograph the runner and crew on the summit
Sports bag	Store mountain gear during the event
Aspirin or supplement for altitude sickness relief such as Altitude Adjust	Minimize the affect of altitude. Altitude Adjust is available at www.runningdelights.com
Crew Gear	
Personal toiletries	Personal hygiene
Clothing for desert such as Sun Precaution Solumbra 30 SPF clothing	Protect skin from sun and heat available at www.sunprecautions.com
Running shoes for pacing	Provide change between running and crewing shoes
Hydration and calories	Maintain/replace fluid and calories used in pacing
Daypack	Contain crew member gear

Prepare the van for optimal function in the ultra by performing the following tasks.

- Marking the vehicle to identify it as an ultra support vehicle so motorists are warned that the vehicle can stop frequently and about crewing activity surrounding the vehicle. Comply with any official ultra race rules for marking crew vehicles and mark crew vehicles supporting solos with a "Caution, Runner on Road" sign that can be seen by approaching traffic when the vehicle is stopped and opened to access crewing gear. Avoid permanence on private vehicles or damage assessments for rental vehicles.
- Ensuring that requirements for character size is met and that the material chosen for the caution sign withstand the heat of Death Valley and can be removed from the van after the event to avoid permanence on private vehicles or damage assessments for rental vehicles. Consider having low-tac vinyl cut or magnetic signs made at a local sign making store.
- Obtaining an extra ignition key or making an extra key storing the extra key on the outside of the vehicle

- Becoming familiar with controls for:
  - Headlights
  - Air conditioning
  - Driver's seat adjustment since multiple drivers will likely drive the van
  - Door locks
  - Handles to slide open and close van doors, tailgate, and/or rear window
- Disengaging automatic or child locks on doors
- Displaying the park entrance permit in the windshield

Organize the crew van as follows.

- Remove and store or fold down the middle bench/row of seats in the van so that only the driver's row and a back row remain. Removing and storing the middle bench from a rental van that you pick up on your way to Death Valley can be difficult. If the van has a luggage rack, the removed seat can be stored there.
- Tape the plastic tarp to the floor of the passenger area of the van to help with cleanup.
- Maintain access to the van from the sliding doors on both sides clear.
- Place and store on the dashboard the marker that is used to identify the point in the desert where the runner takes a break off the course so you know exactly where to return the runner to the course to continue the ultra.
- Use and arrange three coolers as identified in Table 4.

Table 4 — Cooler Uses

#	Purpose	Specifications	Use	Location in the Van
1	Store ice and water for cold drinks	• 5-gal, round NFL type Gatorade-type • Pour spigot • Handles for carrying • Secure lid	• Fill this cooler with one block of ice and one bag of cubes and gallons of bottled water. • Keep this cooler uncontaminated with dirty hands, bottles, etc. • Fill water bottles with drinking water from the melted ice.	• Place this cooler on the floor of the van where it can be accessed from the open sliding door when the van is stopped to crew. • Secure the cooler in place with bungee cords to prevent it from spilling on steep hills and sharp turns. • Place the spigot facing to the outside.
2	"Refrigerator"	• 15-gal, ice chest-type • Elevated shelf to	• Fill this cooler with one block of ice on the bottom and with cube ice but do	• Place in the rear of the van accessible through the

#	Purpose	Specifications	Use	Location in the Van
		keep items dry & separate from melting ice • Drain spigot • Handles for carrying • Secure lid	not bury the cooler contents with the cubes. • Store items requiring refrigeration. • Drain water to use it to fill spay bottles, soak feet, or for any non-potable use. • Replace melted ice drained from the cooler with cubes from the ice storage chest.	hatchback door. • Arrange it with the open lid facing the outside. • Do not store other items on top of it. • Store the funnel and ice scoop in the cooler.
3	Ice storage chest	• 15-gal, ice chest-type • Drain spigot • Spigot for cold water • Handles for carrying • Secure lid latch	• Fill this cooler with a two blocks of ice and the remainder with bags of ice cubes. • Do not open this cooler except to remove ice to re-supply coolers #1 and 2. • Use an ice scoop to fill bottles with ice from the cooler. • Do not store anything in this cooler but the scoop or funnel. • Later in the event, drain this cooler into cooler #1 as a source of cold drinking water.	• Place in the rear of the van accessible through the hatchback door against the back seat bench • Store other frequently used items on top because this cooler is only used as a source to re-supply ice in coolers #1 and 2

To get this massive amount of gear and three crew members into the small space of a van moving through 135 miles of extreme desert temperatures and find all the items, Figure 3 suggests an organization. Here are details to organize all this gear and supplies in the van suggested in the van organization illustration.

- Arrange "kitchen" supplies, medical items, foot care box, and runner gear in easily accessible separate containers as shown in Figure 3.
- Identify a specific place in the van for the container of night gear such as reflective vests, blinking lights, flashlights, and crew headlamps.
- Keep money for ice and gas in the glove box.
- Keep the Death Valley Ultra Notes Template on a clipboard with a pencil or pen attached on a string in the front of the van.
- If the van has a roof rack, use it to store luggage and other travel-related items that are not needed for crewing and that are not affected by exposure to heat.

Place the following largest, most frequently accessed items in the van and ensure that they are secure as the vehicle moves on winding roads and steep hills.

- Front of van—console, dash, board, glove box
  - Death Valley Ultra Template
  - Official race information
  - Camera
  - Bank deposit bag with money, receipts, credit card
- Open area of the van between the front seats and the seat bench
  - Runner's clothing and gear in a sports bag or plastic tub on the seat bench in the back of the van
  - Cases of water under the seat bench
  - Working crew's gear in small back packs on the seat bench
  - Folding lawn chair(s) in a secure space in the
  - Medical supply box on the floor
  - Foot care box on the floor
  - Cooler #1
- In the rear of the van accessible through the hatchback door
  - Boxes with food and kitchen supplies
  - Coolers # 2 and 3
  - Small box of hardware and batteries
  - Container of night gear

5.3 Organizing The Crew Shuttle Vehicle

Prepare the shuttle vehicle for optimal function in the event by:

- Marking the vehicle to identify it as an ultra support vehicle so motorists are warned that the vehicle can stop frequently and about crewing activity surrounding the vehicle. Comply with any official ultra race rules for marking crew vehicles and mark crew vehicles with a "Caution, Runner on Road" sign that can be seen by approaching traffic when the vehicle is stopped and opened to access crewing gear. Ensure that the sinage can be removed from the vehicle after the event to avoid permanence on private vehicles or damage assessments for rental vehicles.

- Obtaining an extra ignition key or making an extra key
- Storing the extra key outside the vehicle
- Becoming familiar with controls for:
  - Headlights
  - Air conditioning
  - Driver's seat adjustment since multiple drivers will likely drive the vehicle
  - Door locks
- Deactivating automatic or child door locks
- Displaying the park entrance permit in the windshield

Figure 3 — Van Organization

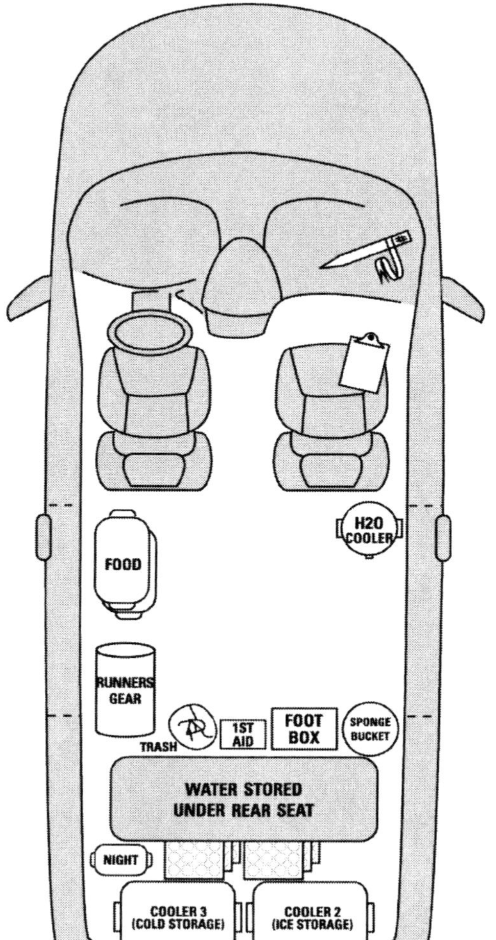

Arrange the trunk and backseat space with the following items:

- Gear for Mt Whitney such as mountain clothes, trekking poles, trail shoes, crampons, mountain food and hydration, etc
- Crew and runner street clothes not used during the event
- Official race packet, i.e., the goodie bag
- Extra cases of water and food supplies that can not fit in the van

It's imperative that the crew van stays organized. If the organization of the van is poor, it is difficult for any crew members to do a good job.

– Denise Jones on crew van organization taught at Ben & Denise Jones

Death Valley ultra clinics since 1994

Chapter 6 — Crewing During The Event

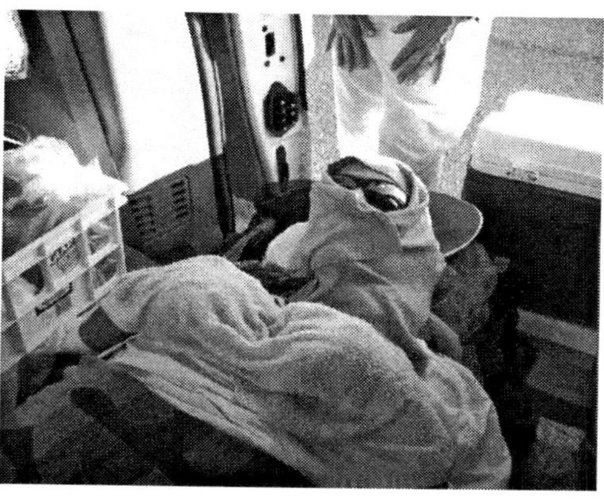

Changes in the runner's physical status can occur very fast in a Death Valley ultra.

The entire Death Valley ultra and the successful outcome is based on a plan prepared for months preceding the ultra that focuses on a future point in time. When executing the plan on the race course, the overriding principal of on-course crewing is to be in the present. This means that crew members take the responsibility for the plan and know it to implement it on time. When crew members take responsibility for the plan, they do not irresponsibly ask the runner the foolish question "How are you feeling?" After running 80+ miles in 110-degree average temperatures with 50 some miles to go, crew should know how the runner is feeling. The ultra isn't long enough for the runner to describe how s/he is feeling.

Think of crewing as the live performance where all of the preparation and planning are applied. This chapter describes the elements of the crewing activities and responsibilities during the event and how to implement the critical teamwork and designated roles that is the crew framework in the following sections:

- 6.1 Knowing Death Valley Ultra Rules
- 6.2 Driving The Crew Vehicles
- 6.3 Administering To The Runner
- 6.4 Managing Breaks
- 6.5 Finishing The Ultra
- 6.6 Being An Effective Crew And Team

6.1 Knowing Death Valley Rules

When Death Valley ultras began in 1977 with Al Arnold's first successful crossing after several unsuccessful attempts, there were no rules only common sense. Because so many runners are inspired by the challenge of Death Valley and attracted to official races, rules of competition exist to safely move the large number of competitors and crews through Death Valley at the same time. While both the runner and crew members are responsible for knowing and implementing the rules, most of the rules rely on the crew to comply with since the runner is occupied with running and is not as lucid as the crew s/he is relying on. But it is the runner who suffers the consequence when crews do not follow official event rules. The consequence can be disqualification from the race and even banning from entering the race in the future.

Check official race information for specific race rules as they can change for numerous reasons. Runners and crews of Death Valley solos should also consider the following list of regulated categories in planning the solo since these categories address important aspects of crew and runner safety, function, and performance as well as compliance with federal agency laws.

- Death Valley National Park rules including rules for commercial recording if applicable
- Highway rules for the pedestrians — the runner and pacers
- Rules about vehicle number, type, size, marking, parking, driving, and locations where vehicles are permitted
- Crew requirements and rules
- Safety rules for runner identification and running at night
- Check point or observation/monitoring/reporting requirements
- United States Forest Service rules for climbing Mt Whitney

Most of the governing rules for solo crossings on the Death Valley course have been in place since the 1970s when the course was first recognized. The rules were codified by The California Ultrarunners Club in the early 1980s and listed in *The Death Valley 300* that documents the first-ever out-and-back crossing of Death Valley from Badwater to Mt Whitney by Tom Crawford and Rich Benyo in 1989. These rules have been updated but without "official" codification. These "rules" for Death Valley ultras that are not part of an official event are not "official" rules, cannot be enforced, and can and will be disputed and revised. But observing the following guideline rules for Badwater to Mt Whitney crossings that do not occur in an official Death Valley ultra event standardizes solo crossing.

Undisputable rules of solo Death Valley ultras include rules of the road for the highways/roads for vehicles/pedestrians, Death Valley National Park rules, and United States Forest Service rules of the trail for Mt Whitney. See Chapter 12 for Mt Whitney permit information.

Crewing During The Event

A summary of the collections of codified and updated guideline rules for Death Valley solos follows.

- Solos must occur between July 1st to August 31st.
- Take a dated photograph to support proof of the start and the finish.
- Solos must begin between 6:00 a.m. and 11:59 a.m. to count as an "a.m. start." Other start times are considered "p.m. starts."
- Crew vehicles are allowed.
- Solo runners may leave the course provided they return to that exact point they left and continue from that point. All time spent off the course is recorded in the total finish time.

Report solo record information to Hugh Murphy at HughMurphy@InyoUltra.com http://inyoultra.com.

6.2 Driving The Crew Vehicles

Because of the extreme temperatures of a Death Valley ultra, the runner is crewed at 1-mile intervals along the entire 135-mile Death Valley ultra course to prevent the runner from being very far from aid at any point during the ultra. A runner's condition can change very quickly and crew need to be very close to the runner to quickly respond to a problem the runner is experiencing or to prevent the problem from developing into a bigger problem.

The road on the Death Valley ultra course is narrow; posing safety challenges to the runner and to drivers parking crew vehicles.

Measure the 1-mile intervals using the tripometer on the van. On State Highway 190/136, the crew van driver can use the highway mile markers to gage the 1-mile intervals. There are mile markers along the road every mile on the half-mile when traveling west and every mile on the mile when traveling east on Highway 190/136. At each mile, the driver drives the van past the runner, finds a safe place to park with all four wheels completely to the right of the white highway line, and the crew crews the runner.

The road on the Death Valley ultra course is narrow with sandy or rocky, and at times non-existent shoulders that make parking a thoughtful process. In general there are turnouts at most mile intervals on the course but these turnouts can have other crew or tourist vehicles parked during a Death Valley ultra.

Do not run the van's air conditioning while crewing except for off-course breaks when the runner needs to cool off in the air conditioned van. To generate air conditioning for this circumstance, after the runner gets in the van and the point of departure from the course is marked, drive the van at highway speed to produce cool air from the air conditioning.

Do not turn off the van while parking to crew but ensure that the van's windows are open in case the doors become locked. A running van that the crew is locked out of is not useful when the runner needs to be crewed promptly every 1 mile and there is no extra time to gain access to the vehicle and all of its contents. The extra key stored on the outside of the van quickly solves this problem.

Table 5 lists common mechanical problems encountered during crewing a Death Valley ultra and strategies to resolve them.

Table 5 — Crew Van Mechanical Problems in Death Valley

Mechanical Problem	Resolution
Overheating the engine when air condition is running because it is not moving fast enough to cool the engine, which in turn causes radiator overflow or worse	Do not run air conditioning off from start: stay hydrated instead of running the air
Running out of gasoline	Fuel before start and at every fueling opportunity
Draining the battery while engine is off at night with interior lights on	If the van has to be turned off for a long break at night, use headlamps or flashlights instead of the van's interior lights and have bug spray available because bug are rampant in Death Valley at night. A battery-operated lantern may be a handy alternative.
Locking keys in the van running or not	Use the extra key secured to the outside of the vehicle when preparing the vehicle the day before the ultra Wait 2, 4, or 8 hours for a tow truck/locksmith Break a window to get access to the vehicle
Auto breakdowns	Have personal vehicles used as crew vehicles serviced before coming to Death Valley
Overheated breaks on steep descents	Downshift on downhills to save the breaks

6.3 Administering To The Runner

Planning and organizing is the majority of crewing but actually administering to the runner during a Death Valley ultra is the core of crewing and the purpose of all the planning and organizing. This section describes the actual crewing process.

Crew the runner on the side of the road s/he is running which is the shoulder facing on coming traffic, the opposite lane from the lane that the van is traveling and parking. Use a tote carrier with handles to carry the numerous items—ice for the hat, ice bandana, food, water bottle, meds, sunglasses, lip moisturizer, etc for crewing from the van to the runner as s/he passes by the van. Wearing shorts with lots of big pockets can be used to carry items required for crewing. One crew member should meet the runner approximately 50 yards before the van and learn from the runner anything that s/he wants in addition to the items planned at the crewing point. The crew member can jog ahead to relay the runner's needs to the other crew member who can get the item from the well organized van and include it in the tote carrier with the other crewing items. Two-way radios with a 2-mile radius can be used between crew members to reduce running back and forth to crew the runner.

While one crew member is crewing the runner — changing the ice bandana putting ice in the hat, changing water bottles, giving the runner food and medications, learning how the runner is feeling, and receiving input for the next crewing encounter, the other crew member with the spray bottle asks the runner if s/he wants sprayed and administers the spray. The "sprayer" crew member picks up any items the runner dropped such as an empty bottle or used ice bandana as s/he passed the van on the sprayer's return to the van.

Be alert to traffic on the road as you cross it. Much of the traffic is tourists who don't know, understand, or care about the race or your focus on crewing the runner.

Details of crewing are described in the following topics:

- 6.3.1 Hydration, Calories, and Electrolyte Management
- 6.3.2 Cooling
- 6.3.3 Managing Health Issues

These topics relate to the crew and pacers as well as the runner although the crew does not experience them in the extreme that the runner does and pacers experience them for a shorter time when pacing.

6.3.1 Hydration, Calories, and Electrolyte Management

Although there are numerous variables to a successful Death Valley ultra, hydration may be the pivotal variable that all the other variables balance. If the runner cannot maintain sufficient hydration to run, the success or even the completion of the ultra is in jeopardy. The variables within the process of hydration are numerous and have a sensitive relationship to each other. Everyone wants a simple answer to hydration — consume X ounces of fluid over Y minutes with a designated dose of electrolytes. Unfortunately hydration in desert endurance sport is not simple. Here are the variables of hydration that have to be recognized and balanced.

- The skin can sweat 3 liters/hour.

- The exertion of running in temperatures over 100 degrees requires fluid intake of 2 liters/hour. In extreme heat, every 15 minutes about a half-liter of fluid should be consumed to prevent a deficit in fluid intake and to establish adequate urinary output.
- The stomach empties at a rate of 1 liter/hour and with heat acclimatization, the stomach can be trained to empty faster, perhaps up to about 2 liters/hour.

Adequate heat training can reduce these figures. Evaporation produced from cooling the runner with water-spraying can take the place of fluid lost through sweating and possibly save about 1 liter of sweat instead of the listed 3 liters, reducing the total to around 2 liters of perspiration.

At times it seems that fluid intake goes straight through to the skin and not to the kidneys. But for consumed fluid with its calories and electrolytes to be beneficial in hydration it has to get from the gut (gastrointestinal tract) to the cells of the internal organs.

It is at this last stop in the organ cells where the essential exchange of electrolytes takes place, particularly sodium and potassium but also calcium and magnesium and other important ions. When the variables are out of balance, the runner's stomach can reject fluid intake. If the cause among theses variables cannot be determined and adjustments made to the hydration and electrolyte intake to prevent the stomach from rejecting intake, the runner will not have the necessary hydration, electrolytes, and calories to run.

Here are considerations about balancing the variables of hydration, calories, and electrolytes.

- The challenge in maintaining calories in a Death Valley ultra is similar to the challenge to take in and process calories over a long period of time while the runner is stressing his/her digestive system with the effort of continuous running. The extra challenge for the runner in a Death Valley ultra is similar to the calorie intake and processing under stress in other ultras plus the stress of the extreme heat. Generally, liquid calories are easier to process than solid food. Solid food may be better able to be consumed and processed when temperatures cool.
- Sports drinks or other products that have various forms of sugar can be difficult for a runner's stomach to process especially in the later stages of the ultra. If the runner plans to use a product for calories with sugar in it have an alternative available.
- A sign of balanced hydration is frequent and clear urination.

- If a runner's stomach rejects something, discontinue using it until after the stomach has stabilized. The quicker the runner's stomach is stabilized, usually by a brief rest from consuming the offending product and taking some salt with plain water, the less dehydrated s/he will become.
- When the runner, crew, or pacer need a break form the ultra food, there are places on the course to get cooked restaurant food. If the runner can eat such food or can be encouraged to eat restaurant food if other calories are not staying in the runner, take out restaurant food may be helpful. Have a crew member procure takeout food from a restaurant on the course. See Table 8 for a list of restaurant locations and availability on the Death Valley ultra course.
- Do not pre-mix large quantities of any powdered drink the runner may be readily consuming. Instantaneously his/her tolerance for it can change and it may be many hours before s/he can use the mixture again. Large quantities of pre-mixed drink takes valuable space in the refrigerator cooler.
- To minimize the runner's stomach processing efforts, open any electrolyte capsules and mix the contents in a drink so the runner doesn't have to use any effort to take capsules or to process them.
- Alternating one bottle of electrolyte/calorie drink with one bottle of water generally is easier for the runner's stomach to process.

The subject of hydration, calories, and electrolyte management is serious and important to a successful Death Valley ultra. For a humorous perspective on this serious subject see Appendix B: Humorous Writings of Ben Jones.

6.3.2 Cooling

Cooling the runner is an important crewing task and can take several forms depending on the runner's preference. But all cooling is dependent on the runner's ability to perform in the heat. Some metabolisms are better than others in the heat, but all benefit from heat training prior to the Death Valley ultra. This section describes considerations about cooling in the following sections:

- 6.3.2.1 Acclimating to Heat
- 6.3.2.2 Cooling Techniques

6.3.2.1 Acclimating To Heat

Here are heat training considerations to implement to maximize performance at a Death Valley ultra and make cooling techniques effective.

Heat acclimatization is necessary for the body to adapt to the extreme temperatures and can take up to 2 weeks. A general rule of heat acclimation is 1 day to acclimate to an additional 3 degrees Fahrenheit. The body's plasma volume expands during this period of time and this increases the ability to sweat and therefore to cool off. The sweat of a heat acclimated runner releases less salt than is lost by a runner who is not heat acclimated. The stomach can expand more and begin to empty faster as the fluids pour in. For heat acclimated runners the sweating seems to become more efficient and perhaps less fluid is lost through the skin and more fluid is provided to the kidneys thereby forming more urine. Ensure that the runner, crew, and pacers are physically capable of heat training, possibly with a medical checkup, before starting heat training activities.

Three weeks is the optimal heat training time with longer heat training periods being more beneficial Spend as much time above 100 degrees F as possible and that means traveling to the low deserts of Southern California or the eastern desert areas such as Panamint Valley and Death Valley. Begin by spending non-exercising time outdoors in these areas and ease into training. Acclimation to heat is possible through passive conditioning, that is, it is possible to become heat acclimated without vigorously exercising in the heat. Estimate how many hours or days it will take to get through the Death Valley ultra and heat train for that projected time period.

Basic heat acclimation can be accomplished in 10 days if the runner is acclimated to running in 90-degree temperatures. Ten days of heat acclimation is based on the 3 degrees per day to achieve acclimation to the 120-degree Death Valley average July through August temperatures. For runners, pacers, and crew who are unable to acclimate in Death Valley, it is possible to simulate effective heat training conditions at home using the following methods.

- Use a sauna that has space to exercise.
- Train in dark clothing worn on the torso and neck trapping the heat during exercise.
- Get in the right frame of mind about running a Death Valley ultra in the heat of Death Valley.

6.3.2.2 Cooling Techniques

Depending on the runner's preferences, here are techniques that the crew can use during a Death Valley ultra to cool the runner.

- Ice bandana around the runner's neck are prepared using a regular cotton bandana and following these steps.

1. Lay the bandana in front of you like a diamond shape on a flat surface such as on one of the coolers.

2. Place about 8 ounces of ice cubes and chips from the "refrigerator" cooler in a horizontal line about 6 inches above the bottom corner of the diamond.

3. Starting at the point furthest away from you, roll the bandana over the ice. Continue until the last corner is rolled into the long tube.

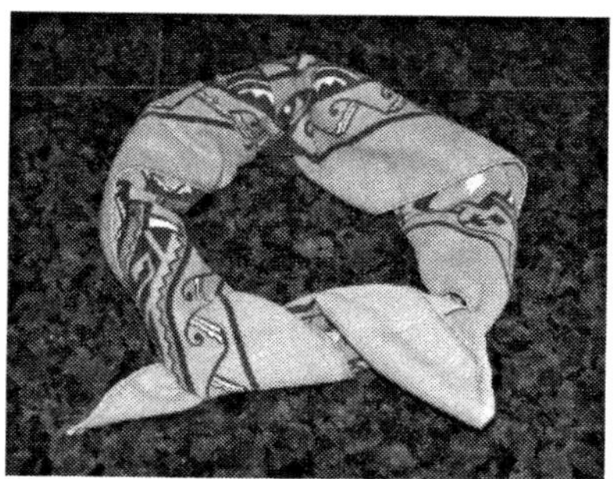

4. Leave about 3 inches on both ends of the roll for the runner to tie around his/her neck.

Avoid the following variations on ice bandanas:

- Bandanas with slots sewn in; they take time to poke the cubes into
- Manufactured chemical neckbands that activate when they are soaked: they are too heavy and not cold enough

Several bandanas can be prepared in advance and stored in a small cooler just for the neck bandanas.

- **Ice in the hat** helps cool the blood going to the brain and provides a evaporative as well as cooling effect to the head that is exposed to the sun and heat. Either dump ice cubes from a plastic cup into the runner's hat or wrap ice cubes in a bandana and place that "packet" in the runner's hat.

- **Wet a chamois or towel** to drape on the runner's head, neck, shoulders, or over the chest while the runner is walking for an evaporative cooling effect or when resting for cooling. Chamois stay wetter longer than towels. To prepare the wet chamois or towel, drain water from melted ice from the spigot of the refrigerator cooler into a bucket or basin over the chamois or towel. Wring excess water from the wet chamois or towel to prevent water dripping on to the runner. Re-wet the chamois or towel in the basin or bucket when it dries, or if the runner prefers, use the sprayer while it is on the runner to rewet the dried towel or chamois.
- **Spray the runner with water** while s/he is running. Fill the spray bottle with water from melted ice from the spigot of the refrigerator cooler. Add ice cubes from the refrigerator cooler if necessary. As the runner approaches, "pre-spray" the ground to remove heated water from the hose or nozzle. As the runner requests, spray the runner's upper body (head, neck, shoulders, chest) as s/he passes through the crewing point. Avoid spraying sunglasses and around the waist, legs, and feet to avoid contributing to sources of chaffing and blisters.
- **Immerse the runner in an ice cooler with water.** Hang the feet outside of the cooler and try to minimize water dripping onto feet and into shoes when the runner gets out of the water. Muscle cramping can occur from getting into the cooler.
- **Air conditioning** in the van can cool the runner taking an off-course break. To generate air conditioning, after the runner gets in the van and the point of departure from the course is marked, drive the van at highway speed to produce cool air from the air conditioning.

6.3.3 Managing Health Issues

There are a variety of health issues that can arise in a Death Valley ultra in addition to the hydration, feeding, and electrolyte related issues. For detailed information to identify, treat, and prevent heat illnesses from exertion in hot environments, refer to *Exertional Heat Illnesses* by Lawrence E. Armstrong.

It is good when the runner describes and reports any health issues s/he is experiencing. Even complaining about discomfort is a better than a disoriented, non-verbal runner unable/incapacitated to describe his/her symptoms. Although runners at times may be less verbal and focusing on the effort and not conversant, question the runner who has not provided feedback for a period about specific symptoms s/he is experiencing. A general "how are you feeling?" question is not helpful for a runner on the edge of a health crisis.

This section identifies conditions from running in heat and treatments administered along the ultra course by the crew.

- **Dehydration** is difficult to determine based on intake and output alone due to the complexity of electrolyte balance and heat effects. If urination has stopped, don't conclude that it is dehydration. Overly hydrated runners may stop urinating. Fluids that are too concentrated may draw water from the blood to stomach, adding to dehydration. Symptom of dehydration include sunken eyes and skin turgor. To test skin turgor, pinch skin on the back of the hand. If the skin sticks together like a tent instead of returning to its natural position the runner can be dehydrated but not necessarily from not drinking. Treat dehydration with water if the runner is processing water.
- **Hyponatremia** (over hydration) can be serious. Symptoms include abdominal cramping and/or vomiting, headache, restlessness, swollen hands and feet, lethargy, confusion, wheezing, slowed breathing, shivering when not cold, increased weight, thirst, incoherence, bloated stomach, muscle cramps, disorientation, inappropriate behavior, puffy fingers and ankles, muscle weakness and/or tremor, malaise, stupor, and slurred speech leading to coma, paralysis, and death. If the skin pinch test described in the dehydration description barely produces a pinch of skin because skin is a boggy, hyponatremia may be indicated. Mental change associated with fluid overload indicates a serious medical emergency. To treat mild hyponatremia, the runner needs to urinate. Stop running and stop drinking water and replace with a concentrated sodium solution such as salty broth to start urination. Severe symptoms require medical attention.
- **Impending heat illness** including heat cramps, heat exhaustion, or heat stroke is characterized by nausea, vomiting, headache, dizziness, faintness, irritability, lassitude, weakness, rapid heart rate, and decreased sweating. Symptoms may progress from minimal to complete collapse in a short period.
- **Heat cramps** symptoms include muscular pain and spasms usually in the abdomen or legs. To treat muscle cramps, get the runner out of heat and cool him/her down, hydrate, and replace potassium.
- **Heat exhaustion** is characterized by cool, pale, moist skin, heavy sweating, dilated pupils, headache, nausea, dizziness, vomiting, with near

normal or moderately elevated body temperature, weakness, lack of coordination, goose bumps, fatigue, and heat cramps. To treat mild heat exhaustion, get the runner out of heat and cool him/her down, lying on the back, with the feet elevated, and remove or loosen heat retaining clothing.

- **Heat stroke** symptoms are the skin is red, hot, and usually dry, pupils are small, high temperature, lethargy, extreme weakness, confusion, odd behavior, disorientation, unconsciousness, and seizures. Heat stroke is life threatening and requires immediate medical treatment. Contact emergency medical services, get the runner out of heat and cool him/her down with ice, air conditioning, wet towels/chamois/sponges. If possible, remove clothing and rub body with ice or immerse runner in cold water. Treat the symptoms similar to a shock victim and do not administer anything by mouth.
- **Nose bleeding** can be caused from the dry Death Valley air. Vaseline applied inside the nostrils can be used as a preventative measure.
- **Nasal congestion** is caused by histamine when water stores drop. Drinking should help this condition.
- **Hypernatremia** (not hyponatremia) is characterized by thirst, dry mouth and mucous membranes, dark urine, loss of skin elasticity, irregular heartbeat, irritability, fatigue, lethargy, labored breathing, muscle twitching and/or seizures. The treatment is to stop running, rest, stop sodium intake, and drink water.
- **Swelling** can be sign of hyponatremia (too much fluid intake), but can also be from too much salt, or pooling of fluid to the feet from the effort of running long distance on pavement. Adjust fluid and/or sodium intake. When the swelling is in the feet, wear a larger size of shoe.
- **Sunburn** can be reduced by sunscreen but sunscreen can diminish the cooling aspects of perspiration. Use sun protective desert clothing.
- **Heat rash and burns** from radiant heat on legs from the pavement. Desitin ointment may alleviate irritation caused by these ailments. Wearing long desert pants can reduce burning on the lower legs cause by the radiant heat from the pavement.
- **Insect stings and bites** can be treated with traditional first aid remedies.

6.4 Managing Breaks

There are several types of breaks from running that a Death Valley ultra may include. Breaks can be for a planned rest and recovery, a psychological break from the pressure and demand of moving through the challenging Death Valley environment, and emergency break to cool a runner near heat stroke, or a quick efficient, "pit stop" to administer to blisters and consume calories and hydration. When a break lasts longer than planned, the runner's pace to achieve his/her goal or to complete the ultra may need to be recalculated. To determine the pace the runner needs to run to achieve a specific time goal or to determine the time a pace will produce, consult the Death Valley Ultra Pace Chart in Appendix C. This chart identifies pace requirements over the last 35 miles of the Death Valley ultra course.

Aspects of breaks that crew are responsible for are described in the following sections:

- 6.4.1 Planned Rest And Recovery Breaks
- 6.4.2 Off-course Breaks
- 6.4.3 Emergency Medical Breaks
- 6.4.4 Withdrawing From The Ultra

6.4.1 Planned Rest And Recovery Breaks

Except for front runners in official Death Valley ultra races, most runners have rest and recovery breaks planned into their paces even if the breaks are crewing breaks and not rest breaks. Some breaks can involve planned sleeping breaks. For runners who have a slower planned pace, rest breaks are part of their strategy for reaching the finish. There are two components of rest and recovery breaks: planning/preparation and efficient implementation.

Rest breaks are scheduled in the runner's plan based on his/her fitness, health, and heat and hill training. Knowledge of the runner's ability, goal, and the Death Valley ultra course are the basis for planning strategic rest and recovery breaks. When planned well, rest and recovery breaks optimize the runner's performance and are a strategic element of a successful race. For example, if the intensity of the heat requires more effort than the return the runner is getting in covering miles, a break from the heat may bring greater returns from a rested runner when the temperature cools.

Planned rest breaks can be motivational for the runner and efficient in meeting the time goal. When the runner knows there is a rest break scheduled for a particular mile or time, s/he can look forward to it and not waste energy or thoughts dreaming of breaks or trying to resist the desire for a break. Likewise the crew doesn't have to wonder about suggesting a break that may not be needed or neglecting a needed break. When the pace drops to a nonproductive level despite the runner's effort, a rest break involving lying down, being motionless, possibly sleeping, carbo-loading, and/or taking caffeine may result in a better finishing time.

Even when a break rejuvenates a runner, s/he will likely experience stiffness when returning to running. Stiffness can be worked through by starting with a slow shuffle until moving overtakes the stiffness. The longer the break the more stiffness the runner experiences.

A planned break can afford a runner the opportunity to:

- Consume a "meal" or a different form of nutrition than s/he consumes while running
- Reload depleted muscle glycogen
- Completely withdraw from the effort and all monitoring questions and stimulation and sleep for a planned period of time
- Change clothes shoes to feel fresher
- Cool off by not working running muscles in the heat

To avoid wasting valuable time and to ensure the break is implemented productively whether it is for sleep and rest or for practical activities such as changing clothes, eating, and foot care, here are guidelines for an efficient break.

- When cooling the runner with wet towels, chamois, or sponges, be careful not to get water in the shoes and socks that can cause blisters or on parts of the body that chafe or clothing that cause chaffing.
- Have supplies identified in Table 6 ready when the break is scheduled; do not make the runner wait while the supplies necessary for the break are prepared.
- Awaken the runner in time to prepare the runner to return to the course within the total planned time period of the break.
- Ensure the runner has all items needed to return to the course such as water bottle, hat, sunglasses, reflective vest, and lighting.
- Secure all items used and return them to their containers in the proper location in the van.
- Collect all trash generated during the break in a trash bag.

- Record all crewing activities, runner input/output, and relevant comments during the break.

The runner's vision for planned breaks are discussed at the pre-event crew meeting and address the elements listed in Table 6. When a pacer is running with a runner, many of the considerations about breaks apply to the pacer.

Table 6 — Planned Break Activities and Required Supplies

Element	Activity Determine if the Runner Will....	Required Supplies Ready for the Break
Rest location	• Lay or sit inside the running van with the air conditioner on • Sit in a lawn chair under any possible shade provided by the van	• Clear space in the van for the runner to sit or lay • When reclining, ensure that the runner does not lay flat: keep the head higher than the heart to prevent the runner from loosing consciousness due to a rapid change in blood pressure and flow • Provide a lawn chair to sit with any possible shade
Foot care	• Elevate his/her feet with shoes on or off • Receive foot care treatment • Change shoes and socks	• Provide an item to elevate the runner's feet that won't be used otherwise during the break — cooler, foot care box, medical supplies box, lawn chair, duffel bags, etc • Place a towel on the ground under the feet for the runner resting outside the van and removing shoes • Ready shoes and socks to change into • Prepare the foot care box for use
Cooling	• Want his/her legs wipe down with cool sponges • Want wet towels applied to the head, shoulders, and torso • Want to use a swimming pool: Runners with taped feet cannot not use this option unless they have time to remove the tape before getting into the pool and then re-taping after the pool session. This is time consuming.	• Wet sponges/chamois/towels in a bucket/basin & wring them out so they are not dripping wet • Prepare items for showering off before entering the pool • Prepare towel, clothing, shoes, and foot care required after getting out of the pool
Massage	• Want a leg massage • Want a foot massage	• If sitting, provide a lawn chair to sit in any possible shade provided by the van • Clear space in the van floor or rear bench for the runner to lay or sit and the person massaging to access the runner • Use lotion on the skin such as sunscreen to reduce friction from massaging
Nutrition & hydration	• Take in nutrition and hydration and the kind nutrition and hydration	• Prepare the "meal" the runner requests • Prepare drinks and water bottles
Quiet time	• Be completely quite and sleep • Listen to music • Chat with crew, media, visitors	• Clear space in the van floor or rear bench for the runner to sit or lay • When reclining, ensure that the runner doe not lay flat: keep the head higher than the heart to prevent the runner from loosing consciousness due to a rapid change in blood pressure and flow

Element	Activity Determine if the Runner Will....	Required Supplies Ready for the Break
		• Provide a lawn chair to sit with shade if possible • Prepare the runner's personal audio device to play music requested by the runner
Clothes & personal care	• Change clothes &/or shoes & socks • Change contacts/glasses • Apply sunscreen/lip moisturizer/eye moisturizer • Answer the call of nature • Take medications	• Ready the clothing, shoes, socks required • Prepare the personal care items that the runner requests
Length of break	• Determine the end of the break himself/herself • Set a time period for the break	• Set alarm/timer on a chronograph • Prepare all items the runner requires to return to the course such as water bottle, hat, sunglasses, reflective vest, and lighting, etc.

6.4.2 Off-course Breaks

Off-course breaks can be planned or they may occur from a break to manage a circumstance usually related to the runner's health condition. Off-course breaks can be part of the planned rest strategy or a strategy to keep a sick or struggling runner in the ultra event. An off-course break usually results in time in a hotel room while emergency off-course breaks may require time spent in the medical facilities provided in an official Death Valley ultra event. The planned off-course break is preferable to an emergency medical break to manage a runner's health situation but you rarely get circumstances to choose between the types of breaks. An emergency off-course break is usually urgent and the only safe choice. All runners from veterans and champions to novices can encounter a situation that requires them to take a break off the course to recover. A runner can successfully finish a Death Valley ultra after a long break or medical attention. A long break is not a reason to withdraw from the ultra.

If an attempt to recover the runner experiencing an emergency health situation by cooling, hydrating, and re-fueling him/her in the air conditioned van is not successful, here are guidelines for an off-course break.

- To cool a resting runner, turn on the van's air conditioning and drive the van to generate more effective air conditioning.
- Before leaving the course, mark the point on the course where the runner is departing to find the exact point when the runner returns.
- At the hotel, continue to cool, rest, hydrate, and get calories in the runner with items from the crew van.

- If the runner is not improving but s/he is not in serious health risk and just needs more time to recover or could recover better in a hotel room, proceed to a hotel room that is reserved for the team.
- If the runner is not improving and is in serious health condition, proceed to medical resources such as those available in an official Death Valley ultra event or to a medical facility.

To return to the course after an off-course break, perform the following tasks.

- Prepare items for the runner's return to the course.
- When the runner is recovered, prepare the runner for returning to the course.
- If necessary, check out of the hotel and ensure all team items are removed from the room and replaced in the crew vehicles.
- Refuel the vehicles and re-supply ice and water if necessary.
- Drive back to the point on the course where the runner left the course.
- Ensure the runner has the items needed to continue on the course — protective clothing, hydration, lighting, etc.

I had a bright idea to try and accomplish the Grand Slam and Badwater in the same season. This was a very difficult task having a new born baby and very little time to train.

Western States 100 went well, Vermont 100 went better than I thought and then 1.5 days later I was standing at the start line of Badwater 135. 110 miles into the race my left foot started to hurt so badly with a bone bruise and a few blisters. Each step was like someone was beating my foot with a hammer. I dropped my flag and had the crew take me to the Dow Villa in Lone Pine. It was about 3 am. I called Denise Jones and she got out of bed and came to look at my foot. It's one of the worst I have ever seen she tells me! I saw my dream fading fast, my body was willing to deal with this foot pain but my mind was not.

Denise saved my race! She found some kind of foot contraption that her husband Ben (Jones) had used in the past and it put my foot in a position where I was not hitting the bone bruise on the bottom of my foot. I went back to my flag and started out very slow and within 30 minutes I was running and walking better than I had the entire race. This was a bitter sweet BW finish for me. I then went on to complete the Grand Slam and Badwater.

Thank you Denise!

Lisa Smith-Batchen
Three-time Badwater Ultramarathon Women's Champion

6.4.3 Emergency Medical Breaks

Medical emergencies can and do occur during Death Valley ultras. When they do occur, it is a serious matter. The ranger staff of the Death Valley National Park is stretched to the limit. When they are off-duty, they are on call for 911 situations. The Park has one rescue vehicle and one ambulance at Furnace Creek. A serious crisis can require both of these vehicles and related personnel. A second crisis at approximately the same time can and has occurred. For very serious problems, Life Flight Helicopter services out of Pahrump, Nevada, can be called and the helicopter meets the ambulance along the way (east of the Park) and then the helicopter service takes the case to one of the hospitals in Las Vegas, Nevada.

> **Death Valley Emergency Phone Numbers**
>
> Emergency phone numbers at facilities in Death Valley route to **911** emergency response in San Bernidino, CA so you only need that one emergency phone number in Death Valley. Here are specific assistance phone numbers.
>
> - Inyo County Sheriff connecting in Independence, CA is 760.878.0383.
> - California Highway Patrol connecting in Bishop, CA is 760.872.5000.

For less serious problems, the local ambulance takes the case west either to Ridgecrest via Trona or to Lone Pine where there are only basic emergency room services. From these two locations, cases are stabilized and then transferred to other more advanced facilities.

The most important device to have is a satellite phone with the local emergency numbers entered into the address book since cell phones don't work well in Death Valley and when they do it is only in a few places. Satellite phones can be rented.

With the large numbers of people involved in an official Death Valley ultra race, an ambulance is present while any runner is in Death Valley National Park that ends at the 85-mile mark on the Death Valley ultra course. Fortunately the ultra course follows the highway through Death Valley and ill or injured runners or crew can be shuttled to the nearest emergency room using the shuttle vehicle.

6.4.4 Withdrawing From The Ultra

Although a runner does not plan to withdraw from the Death Valley ultra that s/he has trained and planned for and converged an entire crew and all of the vehicles, gear, and supplies to remote, challenging Death Valley, a plan for withdrawing from the race must be addressed and discussed in the pre-event meeting with the crew. To ensure that withdrawing from the race is the right strategy at the right time, the runner and crew need to define the following aspects of withdrawing from the race.

- Determine the criteria/circumstances/thresholds that the runner must meet before withdrawing from the race.
- Determine the level of risk the runner is able to accept for the reward of finishing a Death Valley ultra.
- Identify the impact to the runner's health that s/he is willing to accept to meet his/her Death Valley ultra goal.
- Discuss how to identify when the runner has meet the criteria to withdraw.
- Ensure that the crew members know and understand these determinations for withdrawing.
- Do not withdraw from a timed Death Valley ultra event before a cutoff if the criteria are not met. If a runner feels unmotivated, fatigued, overwhelmed, allow him/her to rest until the cutoff. Generally s/he will feel better and re-motivated to get back on the course long before the cutoff occurs. Avoid regretting not finishing by withdrawing too early. If there is time to finish at a point when a healthy runner wants to withdraw, do not make that decision until the time to finish the ultra has passed. For most runners, a longer than planned finish is better than no finish and a better return on the investment s/he has made in the ultra.
- Avoid medical facilities unless there is a true medical reason to use them. A medical environment for a runner who is not in need of medical resources is not a motivating environment.
- Know the location of and access to medical resources that may be required when the runner meets the criteria for withdrawing from a Death Valley ultra.

6.5 Finishing The Ultra

A Death Valley ultra finishes at the Portals of Mt Whitney. The traditional Death Valley crossing is from the lowest point in the western hemisphere where the ultra started at Badwater to the highest point in the continental United States, Mt Whitney at 14, 495 feet, approximately 11 miles above and beyond the finish line and since there is no shuttle service from the summit, the 11 miles back to the trail head. At the finish the runner and crew celebrate the great accomplishment of reaching the finish line, receive awards and the recorded time in an official Death Valley ultra race, take photos to commemorate the accomplishment, thank and hug each other. Sitting and resting to savor the achievement is a good idea also.

At the finish, the crew parks the van at the parking lot of the Mt Whitney Portal among numerous other campers and hikers vehicles. The lower overflow parking lot may be the only parking space available. Due to the distance from the overflow parking to the finish line, be sure that you take all gear needed for the finish from the crew vehicle. Do not leave the van with all of its food and other aromatic contents parked in the parking lot as bear are numerous and cause significant damage when they break into vehicles for food as is their habit at this location.

Here is basic gear to take to the finish:

- Clothing for the runner who has been running through extreme temps for many hours but at the finish is no longer moving and is at an elevation where temperatures are cooler
- A folding lawn chair for the runner to sit
- Lighting for night finishes
- Key to the van
- Camera
- Death Valley Notes Template to record finish time

The next stage of the traditional Death Valley ultra to the top of Mt Whitney begins at this point. The runner and crew have planned the timing of the climb up Mt Whitney as starting directly off the finish line or after a rest, usually at a hotel in Lone Pine. For runners beginning the climb after a rest in a hotel in Lone Pine, drive the van from its parking place to the finish line and assist the runner from the finish line into the van for the drive to Lone Pine. To care for the runner after the Death Valley ultra finish, see Chapter 11.

For runners starting the climb up Mt Whitney directly from the finish line the transition for the crew and the effort for the runner is more difficult than starting after a rest in a hotel in Lone Pine and fewer runners start the climb at this point. Most crews take the runner to a hotel in Lone Pine to administer to the runner, allow him/her to eat and rest while the crew transitions from crewing the desert ultra to climbing Mt Whitney. As part of the transition at the finish line, all food and items that have a scent that attract bear to the van that are parked at the Mt Whitney Portal parking lot for at least half a day must be removed from the van and placed in the bear-proof storage available in the parking lot. It is easier to do all of these tasks at a hotel in Lone Pine. Specifics about preparing to climb Mt Whitney are in Chapter 12.

For runners and crews climbing Mt Whitney directly from the finish line, arrange for the crew shuttle car with the mountain gear and supplies for the mountain to meet the crew at the Mt Whitney Portal parking lot. Clear a space in the van to administer to any of the runner's health/medical needs and for the runner to recline, rest, and eat. Ensure that the rest is timed to allow the team to start the climb at the planned time.

While the runner is resting, the crew prepares gear for the mountain, which is described in Chapter 12. Secure in the bear resistant containers in the parking lot food and items from the van that have an aroma that can attract bear to the crew vehicle. After several days in the desert, nearly everything in the van and shuttle car meets these criteria.

For official Death Valley ultra events, the timing for climbing Mt Whitney is scheduled around the awards ceremony. This important ceremony acknowledges and rewards the accomplishments of participants. All participants, including runners who do not get to complete the official event, should attend with their crews. All participants are recognized and receive an appreciation of what the event is with the contrasts of those who win and those who tried but were not successful in meeting their goal. By attending the ceremony, runners and crew learn of the history of the event, honor champions and finishers receiving their awards, and get a deep appreciation for the challenge of Death Valley ultras.

6.6 Being An Effective Crew And Team

Effective crewing is a combination of understanding, knowledge, and capability. Characteristics of effective crew are listed in Table 2. Understanding the plan that incorporates the runner's goal is the responsibility of effective crew. An effective crew recognizes the crew chief's role and responsibility to make decisions for the entire team. Quick response and efficiency are the hallmark of an effective crew. Even a 1-minute delay in crewing at each crew point in the 135-mile Death Valley ultra results in a 2 hour and 15 minute slower finish time.

Here are crewing techniques that make an effective crew when combined with the overall understanding of the Death Valley ultra, the runner's goal, Death Valley itself, and the crew's role.

- Do not burden the runner with general questions. If crew must ask, ask a question that is easy for the runner to answer and provides specific useful information to the crew about how to manage the situation. Instead of asking, "How do you feel?" when dealing with bloating ask, "Since you took the salt tablet 15-minutes ago, is the fluid processing through your stomach better now?"

- Be in the present. Don't get ahead of the plan. Do not talk about getting a pancake breakfast in 30 miles or what it is like on Whitney that may be a day and a half away. Even when meant as encouragement or motivation for a struggling runner, mentioning distant, upcoming plans can make the runner feel further from his/her goal.
- Motivate the runner. Runner's are motivated by a variety of things that are discussed in the pre-event crew meeting. Motivation is psychological and can be more complex than managing a physical situation such as hydration processing. Despite the preference that the runner be ecstatically happy every step of the 135 Death Valley ultra miles, it's not going to happen. Low moods are reasonable, must be expected. Often they come on very quickly and are amplified in the extremes of the environment and the effort. It's ok for the runner to emote his/her fears, pain, and concerns despite the myth of ultrarunners' stoic acceptance of pain. Struggling is part of the effort of a Death Valley ultra. Recognize that and address runner's concerns practically with reinforcement such as, "Your feet should hurt after what they have been through," or a simple "Yes" acknowledging the reality of the runner's pain. A statement like that from the crew is more realistic and produces a better team outcome than "Quit whining, I'm tired too."
- Crew the crew. When the focus is on the runner and especially in circumstances that the crew is managing a difficult situation that lasts for a length of time, it is easy for the crew to forget about crewing themselves. It is critical to the success of the team that crew maintain their ability to contribute to the effort. If crew members aren't taking care of their own hydration and calories, remind them. Changes in physical status happen very fast in a Death Valley ultra.
- Maintain van organization. The importance of an organized van is critical to effective crewing assuring rotating crew shifts that they know where items are and can get the item to the runner when needed.
- Sort and store food used in crewing. Use zip-lock baggies not the original packaging after food items are opened. Remove as much of the unnecessary packaging as possible when organizing the van to minimize trash.
- Manage trash generated from crewing. An enormous amount of trash is generated from crewing a Death Valley ultra primarily from water

bottles—bottles from the cases of 1-liter water bottles or the 1- and 2.5-gallon water containers. Compact empty bottles, soda cans, and any other trash as they accumulate including the gallon water containers and store trash in a plastic trash bag hung in the van. Dispose of trash every time the crew vehicle is refueled. When a crew member leaves for a rest at a hotel, ensure that the member takes trash to dispose of.

- Handle media who may be on the ultra course during the ultra depending on the runner's goal and interest in the media. A crew member may need to present information about the runner's ultra to the media and provide the media some access to the runner at times that are effective within the runner's race. These times may not coincide with the media representative's interest so managing the media positively and effectively benefits the runner's race without involving the runner or excluding the runner who is interested in media contact.
- Reduce the runner's effort when being crewed. Everything that the crew can do to reduce the runner's effort saves the runner's energy for running. Keep the runner moving while crewing her/him. Here are technique that crew members can use to reduce the runner's effort when being crewed:
    - Cross the road from the van to the side that the runner is running to meet the runner carrying tote carrier with items needed to crew the runner including the water sprayer unless a second crew member is spraying the runner in advance of the runner passing by the van. Sometimes this takes two crew members when it's really hot.
    - Tie and untie handkerchiefs used for neck cooling, but don't trip the runner as you reach in front of him/her.
    - Remove and replace ice hats.
    - After the runner has passed and has been crewed, pick up the water bottle from the ground that the runner has dropped.
    - If acceptable to the runner place any pills s/he takes directly in his/her mouth instead of having the runner focus on the crew member's open hand to get the pills from the hand into his/her mouth. Better yet, open any pills that are in capsule form and put the contents into a water bottle mixture. Be sure the runner drinks the entire contents when you use add the contents of capsules to the drink mixture.
- Use a plastic funnel to scoop ice from the ice cooler, to keep ice clean, and to drain water from the ice before putting the ice in water bottles that have mixed drinks in them to prevent diluting the drink concentration.

- Use a clean ice pick to break up clumps of ice cubes that melt together. Keep it in the ice cooler.
- Manage water in coolers produced by melting ice by draining the water regularly to maximize the cooling effect of the ice in the cooler. Use the drained water as a source of cold water to mix drinks when draining water from the ice cooler and to wet chamois and towels.
- Use water from the cooler for drinking water instead of 1-liter bottles of water to eliminate trash and take less space in the van than cases of bottled water. Use gallons of bottled water to replace water in the drinking water cooler and empty 1 gallon at a time. Crush used gallon containers when they are emptied.

I cannot say enough about the dedication and perseverance of these people who took one to two weeks out of their lives and spent their own time and money support the Badwater Quad. Each crewmember spent a significant amount of time on the course with me, pacing me and generally keeping me moving.

-- Marshall Ulrich, Badwater Quad Record Holder on his motivation for completing his record four crossings of Death Valley to Mt Whitney

Chapter 7 — Foot Care

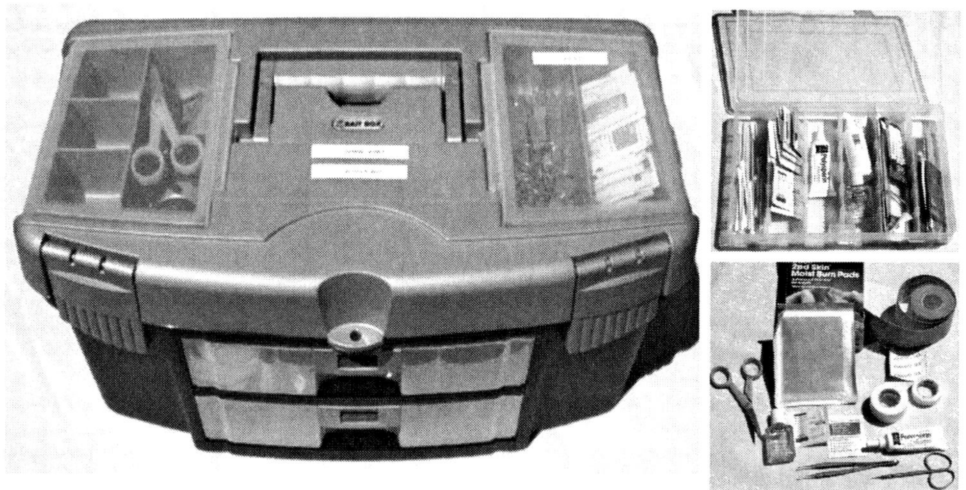

Example of a foot care box equipped with items to prevent and treat blisters.

Blisters are the majority foot care issue in a Death Valley ultra. Most runners drop from Death Valley ultras due to stomach upset or blisters. Blisters are caused by heat friction, moisture, and combinations of these causes. This chapter describes how to prevent and treat blisters that Death Valley ultra runners commonly experience in the following sections:

- 7.1 Assembling The Foot Care Box
- 7.2 Preventing Blisters
- 7.3 Providing Blister Care
- 7.4 Administering Other Foot Care

For a humorous perspective on this serious subject see Appendix B: Humorous Writings of Ben Jones.

7.1 Assembling the Foot Care Box

Assemble a portable, durable, box such as a fishing fly box that can survive use during a Death Valley ultra. The box should have a hinged top, handle for carrying, secure latch closure, and compartments. Equip the box with the foot care treatment items that are listed in Table 7.

Table 7 — Foot Care Box Items

Item	Purpose/Use	Where to Buy the Item
Anti-friction materials		
Tapes • Kinesiotex by 3M - Stretchy, breathable, smooth, non-abrasive 2" width • 0.5" & 1" width Micropore easy to tear paper tape	• Tape large areas and toes • Seal edges of Kinesio tape and can be used on toes for a thin layer	• www.kinesio-tape.com 888-759-7888 • Pharmacy/ Medical Supply • Pharmacy/Medical Supply
Tape Adherent • Tincture of Benzoin • Mastisol	Prep tape to be applied to perimeter around area to be taped	Grocery Store/Pharmacy
Second Skin Burn Gel Two-sided protective prep	Place over blister after draining and before taping	Pharmacy/Medical Supply
Lubricants • Hydropel • Avon Silicone Glove • Body Glide	• Lubricant and to repel moisture and friction • Lubricant to reduce friction • Lube stick to prevent chafing or blisters that can be applied without getting it on hands	• www.hydropel.com or running/adventure racing store • Avon Cosmetic Company • www.bodyguide.com or running shoe store
Between feet and shoe • Injinji socks (Tsoks) • Runner's preferred socks • Balega socks	• Socks that cover toes and foot and separate toes--like gloves for the feet, to prevent blisters and friction between toes • Breathable, absorbent, ant-friction in heat environments • Cushioned running socks	• www.injinji.com/ running store • Runner's gear • www.balega.com/running store
Powders • Blistershield by Two Toms and • Gold Bond Powders • Zeasorb by Stiefel Laboratories	Absorb moisture and prevents blisters • Use to prevent hot spots/blisters; sometimes most effective over lubricant and before socks • Super absorbent powder	• www.twotomslic.com • Drugstore • Drugstore
Shoehorn	Help get a taped or swollen foot back into shoe after treatment	Shoe Store
Vision and Environmental Aids		
Glasses	Vision enhancement for care givers with poor vision	Grocery Store/Pharmacy
Bug spray	Repel bugs during night time foot care	Grocery Store
Headlamp	Provide lighting for night time foot treatment	Sports Store
Foot Care		
Moleskin	Provide padding or support in and around tender areas on foot or deep blisters that cannot be drained	Grocery Store – foot care section
Small, multi-purpose, round-tip utility scissors	Cut tapes	Grocery Store

Item	Purpose/Use	Where to Buy the Item
Sharp surgical or utility scissors	Cut small hole in blister for draining	Medical Supply
Tweezers	Hold roof of blister up to cut a hole into it to drain	Drugstore
Sharps/Lancets	Cut small hole in blister for draining	Medical Supply
Needles	Begin a V-shaped notch in blister for draining	Grocery Store – sewing section
Duoderm burn dressing thicker than Second Skin and sterile	Treatment for serious huge blisters with sterile cover and more padding	Medical Supply
Neosporin antibiotic salve	Apply over open skin or when taping over drained blister	Grocery Store/ Pharmacy
Acetone nail polish remover	Remove reside of tape	Grocery/Pharmacy
Betadyne liquid or wipes	• Clean open wounds or before draining blisters to prevent infection • Similar to Tincture of Benzoin but less smelly and equally a effective	Pharmacy/Medical Supply
Sanitary Precautions		
Disposable, pre-powdered surgical gloves	Provide germ barrier between the patient and the care provider	Pharmacy
Hand sanitizer	Clean the care giver's hands and prevents germs	Grocery Store/Pharmacy
Trash zip lock baggie	Dispose of trash generated during foot care	Grocery Store
Q-tip swabs	Apply alcohol to blister before draining and to apply tape adherent to skin	Pharmacy
2" x 2" gauze	Catch fluid from draining a blister	Grocery Store/Pharmacy
Cotton balls	Apply alcohol to blister before draining and to clean skin and foot care instruments	Grocery Store/Pharmacy
Alcohol wipes	Prep for blisters and hands before treating blisters or any open area	Pharmacy/Medical Supply

7.2 Preventing Blisters

Preventing blisters is the key for a faster and healthier Death Valley ultra because in addition to the pain and discomfort of blisters, it takes time to treat them. The goal should be to prevent them.

The point of preventative foot care is to avoid dealing with blood-blisters or deep blisters and the time to treat them. Tape anything you know has blistered before or is prone to callus. Make sure you have as little callus as possible. Callus is a buildup of dead, thickened skin caused by friction, poorly fitted footgear, and sometimes poor biomechanics. Callus in not a normal condition. Callus needs to be thin enough to penetrate with scissors or a sharp if a blister develops underneath. In the Death Valley heat, feet are subjected to such extreme temperatures from the pavement heat that callus that may prevent blisters in other ultra conditions, is not a suitable protection and difficult to treat and painful when a blister develops underneath it.

The two techniques that are effective in preventing blisters are described in the following sections:

- 7.2.1 Lubricating Plus Toe Socks
- 7.2.2 Taping

7.2.1 Lubricating Plus Toe Socks

The first choice blister prevention technique is an enhanced lubricating method that can work better than pre-taping the feet and is much less time-consuming and requires no training. If this technique is used, taping described in the second technique is not needed unless big areas of the foot are known to blister. Then, tape and also use the following lubricating technique.

1. Cover foot with Hydropel evenly including on and in between toes.
2. Apply foot powder over the Hydropel.
3. Carefully put on Injinji socks onto toes, then onto entire foot, making sure there are no wrinkles in the socks.

7.2.2 Taping

The second technique, to pre-tape the feet the night before the Death Valley ultra, is an effective prevention but requires practice and testing before the event to ensure it is done correctly. A sloppy job of pre-taping is worse than no tape at all, especially on toes. It is possible that the tape applied in pre-taping can last the entire race and may require little treatment through the ultra. The secret of good taping is preventing ridges that can rub any other surface.

Here are steps to tape feet for a Death Valley ultra to prevent blisters. Perform these steps for one foot then repeat them for the other foot.

Preparing to Tape

1. Arrange two seating areas facing each other and the foot care box open and next to the crew member taping the runner's feet. An alternate set up is in motel room where it's cool and have therunner lie on bed face down.
2. Seat the crew member in a chair facing the runner's feet.
3. Clean your hands thoroughly with hand sanitizer or alcohol.

4. Apply Tincture of Benzoin or Mastisol to one foot with Q-tip where edges of tape will be placed — usually on the ball of the foot and on the heel. Do not apply it over the entire area as it is too hard to remove the tape when the whole area is prepped. The tincture can sometimes pull off tender skin when the tape is removed.
5. Allow the tincture to dry few seconds to get tacky before applying tape.
6. Measure areas of the foot to be taped before cutting the Kinesio tape by holding the tape up to the foot with the backing and to "eyeball" the length of tape to be cut.
7. Cut a strip of Kinesio tape based on the eyeballed measurement.
8. Peel off paper backing from the Kinesio tape.
9. Apply the cut strip of Kinesio tape, stretching it slightly. Start on the top edge over top of small toe and extend around the ball of the foot ending on the other side at about the same place but on top of the large toe. Do not tape completely around to where the tape meets itself to prevent constriction when swelling occurs.

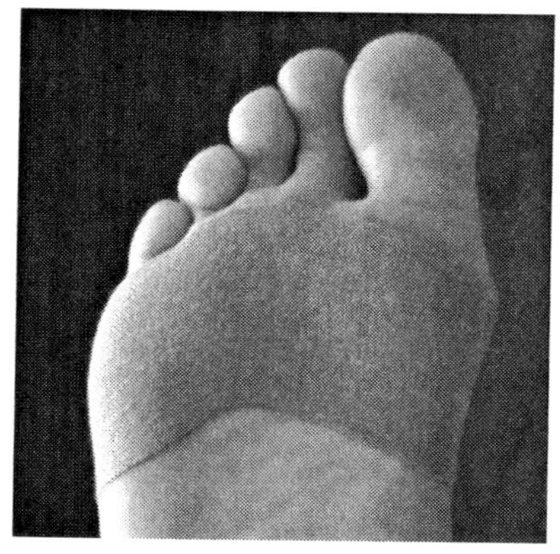

10. Cut two 4" strips of Kinesio-tape for the heels. Apply the cut strip beginning just below the ankle bone and extend around the back of the heel horizontally to the other ankle bone with part of the bottom edge curving underneath heel.

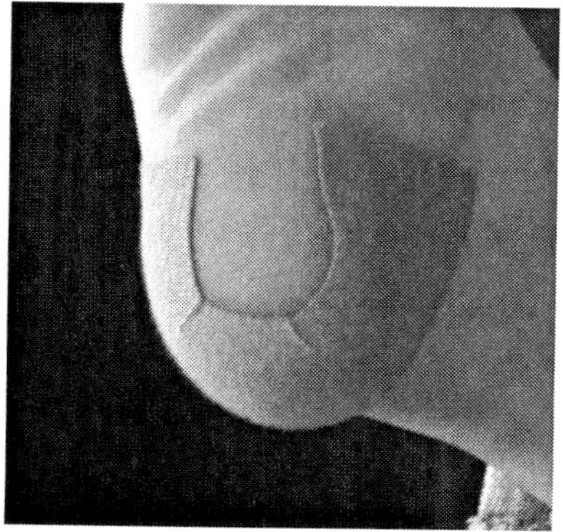

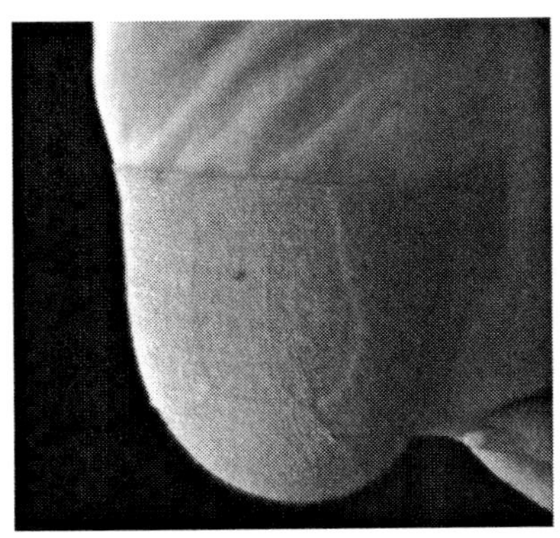

11. Cut one or two 4" strips of Kinesio-tape.
12. Apply one strip to heel from either side of ankle and over the tape just applied around the heel sides. If the entire heel is not covered, tape underneath and around to other side with the second piece of cut tape. If two pieces of tape are used, do not allow gaps so that tape might shift by taping next to the first piece of tape so that no rolling or overlapping occurs.
13. Prep the foot by dipping Q-tip into tape adherent for the final sealing with Micropore tape. Allow to the adherent to dry enough to become tacky.

Taping Toes

14. Cut two horizontal strips of Kinesio tape about 1" to 1.5" long.

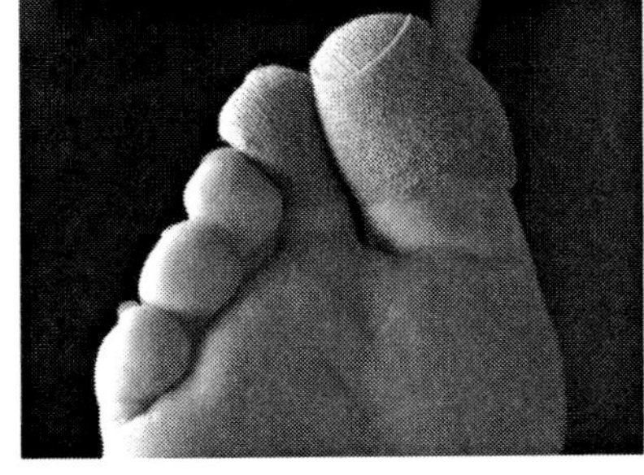

15. Apply tape prep all over toes where tape is to be applied.
16. Apply the half-width (1") length of Kinesio tape starting at the second knuckle of toe, up and over top and ending before second knuckle.
17. Apply the next half-width Kinesio tape around the toe, as if to create a little cover.
18. Trim all edges neatly to prevent blisters from occurring due to rough tape edges.
19. Examine the taping to be sure all edges are sealed with Micropore. Toes may not need sealing since they are so small.

Taping Arches

20. Cut 4" strips of Kinesio tape.

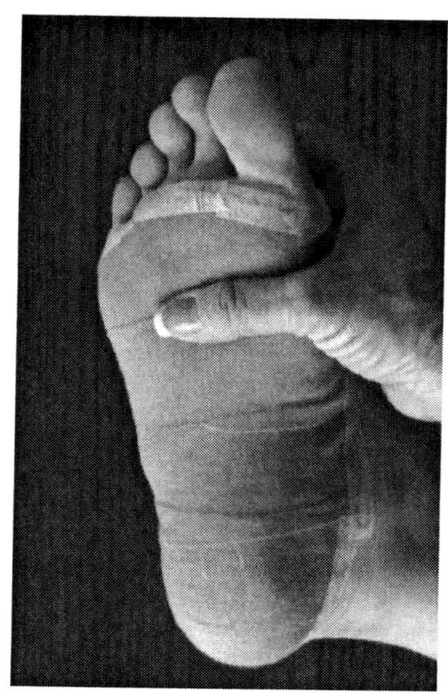

21. Apply tape prep along sides of foot near the arch where tape will be placed.
22. Apply a piece of 4" tape to the next section of foot just forward of the heel tape. Start on the side and pass tape under the sole of the foot and up to the other side. To cover the entire sole, continue this lateral taping until you reach the area where you taped the ball of the foot from ball to heel and up and over the top of the foot to just below the Achilles tendon. Tape from the heel forward when you are taping the whole sole of the foot where the last strip ends to prevent the forward motion of the foot from rolling the tape.
23. Use Tincture of Benzoin around all edges to seal the edges of the Kinesio-tape.
24. After prepping with the tincture, cut or tear multiple pieces of Micropore paper tape of any convenient length to seal the edges of the Kinesio-tape.
25. Check for all edges to be flat and without gaps that skin will squeeze though when foot swells and seal gaps with Micropore tape.
26. Put on Injinji socks over the taped feet and have the runner sleep in them the night before the Death Valley ultra to help the tape mold to the feet.
27. Check foot in morning before event to make sure all edges are secure.

Finishing

The morning of the ultra, perform the following steps.

28. Remove socks from the taped feet to check for any wrinkling or loose edges.
29. Re-seal any wrinkles or loose edges with tincture of Benzoin.
30. Apply Hydropel on areas not covered with tape.
31. Apply powder over Hydropel.

32. Apply an ultra thin sock over the Injinji's if a runner's feet lack sufficient fat pads. Fat pad atrophy occurs most often in older runners who have pounded them away.
33. Clean tools used to tape the feet.
34. Contain trash generated from taping in a zip-lock bag and dispose of it.
35. Reassemble and re-supply the foot care box.

7.3 Providing Blister Care

The extreme heat, perspiration, and constant motion that a runner's feet experiences in a Death Valley ultra commonly cause blisters despite preventive taping of the feet. When a runner experiences blisters during a Death Valley ultra event, the crew member assigned to foot care must prepare to treat the runner's blisters. Prepare a strategy for foot care on the Death Valley ultra course before the race and when the runner notifies the crew that s/he requires foot care, the crew is able to respond with a foot care set up at the following crewing point.

It is often awkward, hot, and painful to have to treat a blister on the course during the race. Prevention is the better option. Here are the steps to treat blisters that occur in a Death Valley ultra.

Preparing the Foot Care Area

1. Park the van shade if possible or in a manner to create shade. Do not make the runner cover additional, unnecessary distance to get to the foot care area.
2. Place an open lawn chair facing where the runner will sit in the sliding door opening on the side of van.
3. Place the foot care box along side the lawn chair.
4. Tape an opened zip-lock baggie to the foot box for trash.
5. Direct the runner to sit in the sliding door opening on the side of van.
6. Maximize the foot care break by crewing the runner with food and fluids and cooling.

Treating Blisters

This technique for blister treatment brings a great deal of comfort to a runner allowing him/her to continue running without the pain caused by a full and growing blistered area. If the runner has more than one blister, treating the worst blister first can bring relief to the pain sooner.

Here are the steps to apply the blister treatment.

Foot Care

1. Clean the hands of the crew member administering the foot care using hand sanitizer or alcohol or wear surgical gloves to prevent infection.
2. Lift the runner's leg to reach the affected foot as little as possible and support them to prevent cramping to sore runner legs.
3. Disinfect blistered area with a cotton ball dipped in alcohol, alcohol swipe, or Betadyne to prevent infection.
4. If the blistered area is taped, remove/cut away any existing tape from the area causing the runner pain. Be careful not to pull tape off quickly or skin on the roof of the blister can come with it. Hold surrounding skin down as you pull tape off gently. Acetone may be used to rid the foot of tape residue.
5. Hold roof of blister up with tweezers and cut a hole with a sharp, lancet, or surgical scissors to drain the blister by making V-shaped notch in blister on the side so that back and forth motion of running stride does not increase likelihood of losing the roof of blister. The notch should be small, but large enough so that the skin cannot reseal to itself. Do not poke hole in blister, it will refill and need more treatment. Try to keep the roof of the blister in tact as protection against infection. If it has torn off, cut it away. Avoid the skin underneath the lost blister roof as it is tender and painful.
6. Drain fluid into 2" x 2" gauze pad then dispose of it in the zip-lock baggie taped to foot box.
7. Apply Neosporin or antibiotic salve to the drained blister.
8. With utility scissors cut Second Skin burn gel in the exact size of the blister and apply it over the top of the blister.
9. Apply Tincture or Mastisol with a Q-tip around the perimeter of patched blister.
10. Apply Kinesio tape over area.
11. Apply Micropore tape around edges of the patch to prevent the tape from rolling or shifting.
12. Clean foot, re-apply Hydropel, powder, and clean socks.
13. Change shoes if they are contributing to the cause of the blisters.
14. Ask the runner to pay attention to any further hot spots, as they are a precursor to blisters and to alert crew if they become problematic.

7.4 Administering Other Foot Care

In addition blisters, there are other foot ailments in a Death Valley ultra that the runner can experience. Here are some considerations to address foot problems other than blisters.

Ben Jones

Practice blister treatment so it can be done as quickly and as well as possible so the runner can return to the ultra promptly.

- Get regular pedicures prior to the ultra to keep feet conditioned but ensure the technician does not file callus with a metal file or shave callus. Metal files and knives take callus down too quickly and can result in very sore and tender feet.
- Make sure shoes and insoles have no rough edges inside.
- Accommodate swollen feet in a larger size pair of running shoes.
- Use various models of running shoes to change impact to the feet. Some shoes can provide support or cushioning for tired, sore feet while lighter running shoes can assist with cooling and drying the feet.
- Pad/protect/cushion sore feet with moleskin or take the pressure off of blisters that cannot be drained. Cut a doughnut hole in a square of moleskin so that the blister fits in the hole and the moleskin surrounds it. Use the sticky side of moleskin to adhere to the foot.
- Use sports sandals if feet get too sore in running shoes.
- Cut part of the shoe away for relief from a painful area where friction is occurring.
- Keep feet as dry as possible avoid immersing feet in water.
- Avoid the feet when spraying the runner for cooling as wet feed can mascerate (become soggy) and blister easier in wet shoes.

Desert Foot Care Don't

- Don't trim callus before taping feet. Reduce callus over time **before** arriving at the Death Valley ultra event.
- Don't start the ultra with toenails that are too long or too thick as these conditions can cause blisters under the nail. Before the ultra trim nails short and square and file thick nails to be thinner and less likely to catch on the upper of the shoe.
- Don't run in shoes with too short or tight toe boxes to prevent a source of friction that causes blisters. If the runner can feel his/her toes against the end of the toe box, then the shoes are too short.
- Avoid cotton socks since they do not wick perspiration and they retain moisture and bunch and stretch creating a source for blisters. Use technical fabric socks that fit snuggly, without seams that rub, especially around the toes.
- Don't use duct tape on feet in the Death Valley ultra since it does not breathe filling the skin beneath the tape with fluid contributing to blisters. When duct tape is removed, the underlying skin is removed with the tape which is painful and dangerous.
- Don't use a pinhole to drain a blister since holes tend to reseal and the blister to re-fill.
- Avoid removing the roof of the blister to minimize infection. If the roof is loose, cut away any flapped skin, clean with alcohol wipes or Betadyne, apply antibiotic salve over it, and dress it with burn gel and tape.
- Avoid draining blood blisters since blood blisters are deeper in the dermis layer of the skin which leads to the blood system. Pad around a blood blister with moleskin and try to keep the blister in tact. Blood blisters often develop when a runner continues to run on a blister until it progressed to the deeper skin.
- Avoid using Vaseline for a lube since it melts in the desert heat. Use non-petroleum based lubricants such as Hydropel, Blistershield Body Glide, or Sports Slick.

Foot Care

Good foot care is one tool that allows <runners> to focus on moving. Some runners are able to maintain such a high state of mental toughness that they continue through the pain of blisters and raw skin when they open, even to the point of bleeding. They are able to detach themselves from the pain and only stop when they are at the finish line

John Vonhof author of

Fixing Your Feet: Prevention and Treatments for Athletes

www.fixingyourfeet.com

Chapter 8 — Re-supplying

Planning well, re-supplying intelligently, and being lucky reduce the chances of running out of priceless supplies.

The remote, extreme environment of Death Valley that offers the appeal and the challenge to runners also offers limited commercial resources. Official ultra events in Death Valley that bring many runners and their crews into Death Valley, impact the availability of consumable items needed for the ultra. Solos during the July to August window compete for supplies with many vacationing international tourists and auto manufactures' engineers testing their designs in extreme environments. This chapter provides considerations for re-supplying consumable supplies--ice, water, and gas used on the Death Valley ultra course and information about re-supply locations.

At times during the summer in Death Valley, ice and gas cannot be bought at any price and crews have to retreat to Beatty, Nevada 35 miles from about the 28-mile mark and the 35-mile mark on the ultra course to the east or to Ridgecrest, CA 79 miles to the south from the 69-mile mark or move forward on the course to Lone Pine at mile 122 to get supplies.

The crew shuttle vehicle can store consumable resupplies such as water and nonperishable food that cannot fit into the van. Re-supply locations and the resources available at these locations are described in Table 8.

Table 8 — Re-supply Locations on Death Valley Ultra Course

Location	Mile	Resource	Hours of Operation	Comment
Furnace Creek	17.6	• General store	• 7:00am to 9:00pm	• The small store sells ice, water, limited groceries, and souvenirs
		• Restaurant	• 6:30am to 10:00pm	• Serves buffet meals for breakfast, lunch, and dinner. A bar is open during the day and in the evening
		• 4-pump/8 nozzle Chevron gas station	• 24-hours credit card pay at the pump	• Oil can be purchased when gas station is open 7:00am to 9:00pm
		• Self-service ice house	• 24-hours	• Requires two $1 US for 5-pound bag or block ice
Stovepipe Wells Village	42	• General store	• 7:00am to 9:00pm	• The small store sells ice, water, limited groceries, and souvenirs
		• Restaurant and bar	• 7:00am to 9:00pm	• Serves breakfast, lunch and dinner menu

Location	Mile	Resource	Hours of Operation	Comment
		• 2-pump/4 nozzle gas station	• 24-hours credit card pay at the pump	• Oil can be purchased when gas station is open 7:00am to 9:00pm
Panamint Springs Resort	72	• Restaurant with ice and snacks for sale • 2-pump/4 nozzle Shell gas station	• 7:00am to 9:00pm • 24-hours credit card pay at the pump	• Power failures affect ice production and fuel pump function
Town of Lone Pine	122	• Restaurants • Grocery • Numerous gas stations with convenience stores	• High Sierra Café is open 24-hours • Joseph's Bi-Rite open 7:00am to 8:00pm • Lees Chevron open 24 hours for gas and Minimart open 6:00am to-8:00pm • AM-PM Exxon and Mobil open 24-hours	• McDonalds and Carl's Jr. from 6:00am to 10:00pm; High Sierra Café, Totem Café, Bonanza (Mexican food) open for breakfast, lunch and dinner; fine dining available at Seasons and Merry-Go-Round • Groceries and ice • Groceries, ice, and some prepared food
Whitney Portals Store	135	• Small restaurant and convenience store snack items	• Open 8:00am to 8:00pm	• Serves limited menu and knows for it large-size pancakes

These resources and hours of operation are correct as of printing but can change or may not be available due to other circumstances.

Planning for re-supply is important but re-supply at any opportunity that arises. If the runner is participating in an official Death Valley ultra with other runners, resupplies of ice and water may be available from crews whose runners withdraw from the ultra.

A Death Valley ultra like much of life is an adventure in focusing and overcoming what life tosses at you. Whether it is in foot care, mental toughness, or any other element of adventure racing, your training helps you prepare for your next event. Just like life itself. Each day is a preparation for the next day.

John Vonhof author of

Fixing Your Feet: Prevention and Treatments for Athletes

www.fixingyourfeet.com

Chapter 9 — Recording The Event

Whether the Death Valley ultra is a once in a life time event for the runner or the beginning, middle, or end of a tradition, the runner's event should be recorded. This chapter describes how to record a Death Valley ultra in the following sections.

- 9.1 Using The Death Valley Ultra Notes Template
- 9.2 Photographic And Video Recording

9.1 Using The Death Valley Ultra Notes Template

A Death Valley ultra last too long for any crew member to remember when all the essential electrolytes, rest periods, medications, etc are administered to the runner. So, use the Death Valley Ultra Notes Template shown in Figure 4 to record information about the runner's event to ensure that the runner is getting the calories, hydration, electrolytes, rest, and meds as planned or as the situation comes to require.

The crew chief is generally the one who maintains this record. Record all relevant information to the runner's race and crewing. At a minimum, record the following information:

- Time and mile crewing activities occur
- Type and amount of calories consumed including restaurant food
- Type and amount of hydration intake
- Type and amount of medications
- Foot care treatment
- Runner's elimination/output
- Comments about anything the runner asks for that is not part of the plan, any comments made by the runner — good, bad, or ugly, or crew comments
- Temperature reading from the vehicle thermometer
- Breaks and activities that occurred during the break to recover the runner

Here are tips for recording.

- Attach the template to the clipboard and tie a pen to the clipboard.
- Store the clipboard in the same place in the van near the passenger seat.

Figure 4 — Death Valley Ultra Notes Template

Jane Smith ***Death Valley Ultra*** ***July 12 – 14, 200__***						
Day, Time	***Mile***	***Fluid/Calories Ingested***	***Meds***	***Runner's Status***	***Comments***	***Temp***
10:10 am	18	8 oz of water	Visine	Sprayed her shoulders & arms	She wants 1/2 nutrition bar the next time	109
10:22 am	19	8 oz of carb drink mixed with water 1/2 nutrition bar	1 electro-lyte pill	Gave her a refreshed ice bandana	She said her knee quit hurting! Yippee!	109

- Make an entry immediately at the end of each crew stop--yes at each mile, while the vehicle is moving to the next stop.
- Consult with other crew members, especially the crew member who had contact with the runner about what the runner said, requested, took of what was offered in accordance with the fueling and hydration plan and cooling.
- Unless all crew members are readily familiar with using a 24-hour clock, do not record time on the template using military time.
- When you return home, transfer the notes into an electric format and distribute the draft to the team to review for corrections or additions. Compile the final edits and distribute the final to the team.
- Treat the detailed race record produced by the notes template as confidential as it details your race plan and how it was implemented.

When the event is complete, use these recorded event notes to:

- Analyze the good and other aspects of the runner's event.
- Help plan future Death Valley ultras.
- Provide information for press releases, event stories, and refreshed memories.

9.2 Photographic And Video Recording

Death Valley and Mt Whitney offers spectacular views and unique photo opportunities. If your schedule and budget allow, spend extra time exploring. Most of the popular Death Valley views are easily accessible by paved road and a short walk. Zabriskie Point, north of the Death Valley ultra course is one of Death Valley's most notable landmarks and worth visiting. Whether photographing during a Death Valley ultra or when touring the scenic valley before or after the ultra, do not block or impede traffic. Traffic moves fast on the desolate roads in Death Valley, and tourists as well as crews can be distracted by the sights, so be careful.

Sunrise and sunset are spectacular in Death Valley. For the best results, turn the flash off, and hold very still. During the day, get good, close-up pictures of people. A fill-flash can help fill in under the shade of a hat.

9.2.1 Ultra Photography

Being part of a Death Valley ultra has some surreal aspects and taking memorable photos help preserve those moments. To memorialize the Death Valley ultra, take photos of the runner and fellow crew at a Death Valley ultra but only when all crewing tasks are complete. Crewing the runner is always the first priority. Don't interrupt the ultra to request a posed photo. Perhaps the best photos may be the candid photos but be respectful of the runner and his/her effort and suffering.

Small digital cameras do a good job of taking snapshots, but be sure to take extra batteries and enough media cards. Plan ahead, and know how many images fit on a media card. While many small (low quality) images fit on your memory card, these low resolution photos aren't great for making prints or for use by the media. Shoot as large (high quality) an image as memory card can hold to make prints that look good.

Night photos are challenging. Reflective vests and signs bounce back a lot of light, leaving everything else too dark. For night photos, be sure to get close enough for the flash to light up the subject. If your subject is out of the flashes effective range, the photos don't turn out well.

9.2.2 Commercial Videography

Death Valley National Park has rules requiring permits for news and promotional videography and official events have their own set of rules about media coverage. If the runner is to be accompanied by media, inquire with Death Valley National Park.

Death Valley National Park
PO Box 579
Death Valley, CA 92328-0570
DEVA_Superintendent@nps.gov
Phone: 760-786-2331
Fax: 760-786-3283
Commercial Permits: 760-786-3241

Even though official Death Valley ultra events are competitive, crews and runners help each other. Ultrarunning is a close-knit community of runners who challenge themselves to personal bests, most without any chance of ever winning an event. There is also no dishonor in helping a member of another team or in sharing secrets with other racers. This is a good way to further your knowledge base.

John Vonhof author of

Fixing Your Feet: Prevention and Treatments for Athletes.

www.fixingyourfeet.com

Chapter 10 — Using Pacers

At a Death Valley ultra, pacers are not necessary for traditional pacing functions of:

- Providing assistance in finding a trail course
- Assisting the runner from getting lost on a trail course
- Carrying gear for miles between aid stations

Pacers must be crewed also.

Runners who are attracted to a Death Valley ultra are usually goal-oriented and independent and don't have much need for pacers on the course. Gratuitously using pacers when they are not needed adds to the logistical plans, use supplies more quickly, and increase the effort of the remaining crew who must provide double crew duties when there is a pacer on the course. Likewise, a pacer gratuitously pacing for his/her own benefit/needs is not helpful to the runner and may be distracting or draining for the runner. Crewing is hard work and pacing can be a fun break but pacing should only be done for the runner's benefit not for a tired crew member's daily exercise quotient. Use pacers when:

- The runner is at a psychological low point that responds to company
- At night to help with fatigue
- The runner is struggling with heat effects and the pacer can alleviate them by accompanying the runner and spraying him/her with water if this type of pacing is permitted by race rules in official Death Valley ultras.

When the runner decides to use a pacer, the pacer must observe Death Valley Park and California Highway safety rules typically running outside of the white line on the highway shoulder and preferably behind the runner.

> *"Badwater is a mental event. . . . the whole distance is on pavement, all on the same side of the road. It becomes a matter of one foot in front of the other. Repeat and then repeat over and over for 135 miles. When the mind says, "Stop," the runner has to use everything available to them to overcome the mind's advice to quit.*
>
> *John Vonhof author of*
>
> *Fixing Your Feet: Prevention and Treatments for Athlete*
>
> www.fixingyourfeet.com

Chapter 11 — Cleaning Up After The Event

After the thrill of completing the desert portion of a Death Valley ultra; achieving the runner's goal; finishing a great desert adventure in a unique, extreme, natural environment; days of adrenaline, hard work, and fun comes the clean up. Naturally the crew would like to celebrate and they deserve a break from their days of effort but letting a van that was home to an average of four people over 2 days smolder in 115 degree temperatures is not a good idea. If the runner is taking a break between the finish of the ultra and summitting Mt Whitney, take the runner from finish line to a hotel in Lone Pine where you should have reservations for the day the ultra is scheduled to be completed. If the runner is going directly from the finish line to the summit, see Chapter 12 for guidelines to prepare to summit Whitney. At the hotel, three major tasks have to happen:

- The runner has to be cleaned up, cared for, fed, and rested.
- The van must be cleaned.
- The crew must prepare to summit Whitney in a few hours.

This chapter describes how to clean up after crewing a Death Valley ultra in the following sections:

- 11.1 Taking Care Of The Runner
- 11.2 Cleaning The Van
- 11.3 Updating The Media
- 11.4 Post-event Paperwork Administration

11.1 Taking Care Of The Runner

For efficiency and in the interest of getting as much rest as possible for all members of the team when the tasks are completed, these tasks can occur concurrently. To accomplish these tasks concurrently the crew chief designates crew members to complete the following tasks.

- Assist the runner with any of the following tasks that s/he needs assistance:
    - Showering
    - Foot care treatment
    - Resting
    - Feeding and hydrating
- Clean the van as described in Section 11.2.

- Contact any media about the runner's ultra results as described in Section 11.3.
- Obtain restaurant food for the team.

11.2 Cleaning The Van

Cleaning the van can be an undesirable task for fatigued crew members who are more interested in celebrating the accomplishment of the ultra finish. But to use the van to transport the entire team and all of their mountain gear the 13 miles to and from the Mt Whitney Trailhead and prevent bear attracted to scents of food from invading the van while it is parked at the Whitney Portals parking lot, the van has to be cleaned at this time. To clean the van, perform the following tasks.

- Take the following items into the runner's hotel room:
  - Foot care and medical boxes
  - Runner's gear
  - Food or drinks the runner needs
- Remove all items from the van and store them in the hotel rooms while the van is in use for the Mt Whitney summit.
- Empty and drain all coolers.
- Refrigerate in the hotel room any perishable food items that the crew will use before or after summiting Mt Whitney or before departing from Lone Pine to return home.
- Use any food items that are appropriate for the Mt Whitney summit (See Section 12.4.)
- Dispose of all perishable food items that will not be used.
- Remove and dispose of all trash from the van.
- Remove the plastic tarp taped to the floor of the passenger area of the van.
- Remove any official race required identification from the crew vehicles.
- Allow no aromatic items to remain in the van since aroma attracts bears when the van is parked at the Whitney Portals parking lot while the team is summiting Mt Whitney.

From the shuttle vehicle, move the following items into the cool hotel rooms:

- Extra food and drinks that was not used during the ultra

- All mountain gear
- All crew and runner non-running personal gear

11.3 Updating The Media

For runners who have established relationships with their local media associated with their Death Valley ultra and with the media that may be on the ultra course with them throughout the ultra, report the runner's finish and finish statistics to those media. For media interviews at the finish, counsel the runner to avoid statements about his/her future Death Valley ultra plans — such as statements that s/he will never run another desert ultra or that s/he can't wait to do one next year. The emotion of he finish is not a good time to attempt to state future running plans to the media.

In statements to media who are not present at the ultra, include the following information:

- Repeat the description of the ultra and the venue previously provided in press releases or interviews conducted before departing for the ultra
- The runner's name
- Finish time and date
- Position in the official ultra race if applicable
- The date line of Lone Pine, California
- Highlights of the ultra
- Death Valley weather conditions
- Notice of the Mt Whitney summit attempt
- High resolution digital photos of the finish with a descriptive caption of who is in the photo and where it was taken
- Quote from the runner about his/her finish and ultra experience

11.4 Post-event Paperwork Administration

Although the team is likely not interested in paperwork after the sports adventure of the Death Valley ultra and Mt Whitney summit, after the ultra and the summit, the crew member functioning as the team "accountant" should collect all receipts for purchases related to the ultra and make arrangements for reimbursing crew members for agreed on reimbursable expenses. It is more difficult to collect receipts and make reimbursements after crew members and the runner return home than it is when the transactions can be done in person before departing.

Cleaning Up After The Event

Don't procrastinate doing this task as expenses and reimbursements can be forgotten as time passes and the team disburses.

Within a week from when the team returns home and has time to process the event, schedule a debriefing meeting for the team to identify the good aspects of the ultra and the aspects that need improvement. The finalized Death Valley Notes described in Section 9.1 can be a catalyst for identifying these aspects. Depending on locations of team members and resources, the meeting can be an in-person meeting, virtual, a teleconference, or other media that the team has access to.

> *"Believe it or not, the two (crew members) that are on duty will be very busy almost nonstop."*
>
> *Mike Henebry, author of "Running Badwater"*

Chapter 12 — Crewing For Mt Whitney

The traditional Death Valley crossing starts at Badwater, the lowest point in the western hemisphere and ended at the summit of Mt Whitney, the highest point in the continental United States. In addition to the challenge of running 135 miles across the hottest place in the Americas when running a Death Valley ultra, the achievement of running from the lowest to the highest points appeals to adventure seeking ultrarunners. The contrast of having these two geographic extremes so close is rare and runners can include summiting Mt Whitney at the end of their Death Valley ultra. To record this accomplishment, report the total lapsed time of your Death Valley ultra from the start at Badwater to the summit of Mt Whitney to Hugh Murphy at HughMurphy@InyoUltra.com or through http://inyoultra.com.

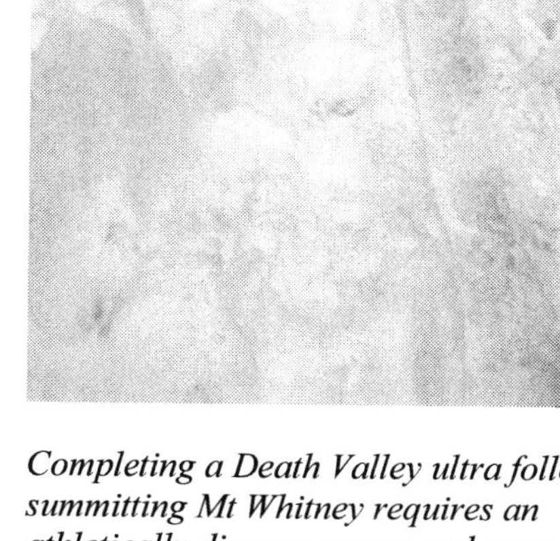

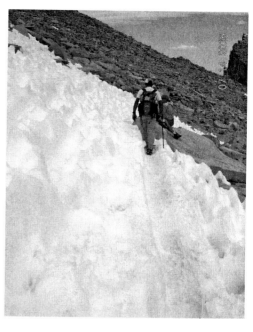

Completing a Death Valley ultra followed by summitting Mt Whitney requires an athletically diverse runner and crew.

Because the United States Forest Service that manages Mt Whitney use and access does not permit races on Mt Whitney, official Death Valley ultra races cannot include this last 11 miles of the challenge and the official events must finish at the end of the Mt Whitney Portal Road. But with a permit purchased from the Forest Service in advance, runners can continue on the remainder of the classic Death Valley ultra.

This chapter describes Mt Whitney and how to crew a runner through the climb after running a Death Valley ultra in the following sections:

- 12.1 About Mt Whitney
- 12.2 Altitude Training And Acclimation
- 12.3 Knowing Altitude Sickness Symptoms
- 12.4 Preparing To Climb Mt Whitney
- 12.5 Crewing On Mt Whitney

12.1 About Mt Whitney

The easiest route up Mt. Whitney is the 11-mile, 6,200-foot hiking trail that starts at the end of the Mt Whitney Portal Road. The trailhead starting elevation is 8,360 feet and the summit at 14,495 feet. A more strenuous mountaineering route (Class 2 to 3) that is not recommended for runners with sore feet or other effects from running across Death Valley just hours before, branches off the hiking trail near the start of the trail. The milestones on Mt Whitney's hiking trail, locations, and elevations are listed in Table 9.

Table 9 — Mt Whitney Milestone Descriptions

Mile	Location	Elevation in Feet
0.0	Trailhead	8,360
0.85	Enter John Muir Wilderness Sign	
2.7	Lone Pine Creek crossing and trail forks to Lone Pine Lake on left and the right continues to the summit	9,980
3.5	Outpost Camp with solar latrine	10,360
4.0	Mirror Lake	10,640
4.9	Approximate beginning of treeeline	
5.0	Trailside Meadow	11,395
6.0	Trail Camp with solar latrine, a lake to extract water for the second half of the climb, and the beginning of 96 switchbacks to Trail Crest.	12,039
8.5	Cross Trail Crest and enter Sequoia National Park	13,777
9.0	John Muir Trail joins from the west	13,480
10.5	Keeler Needle	14,003
11.0	Mt. Whitney summit	14, 495

12.2 Altitude Training And Acclimation

Most people are affected by the reduced amount of oxygen at the elevation of Mt. Whitney but acclimation helps minimize altitude sickness though altitude sickness can strike anyone, even experienced mountaineers. For runners, crew, and pacers who have access to altitude training, training a day at each 1,000 feet above the level that you are acclimated. If you live and train at sea level, you would need approximately 14 days with each day at a progressively higher 1,000 feet of elevation to prepare for climbing Mt Whitney. Altitude training familiarizes the runner to better endure the impacts of altitude. It doesn't make him/her able to overcome the affects of altitude. Here are points about running at altitude.

- A runner can minimize--not change the affects of altitude with overall fitness and strength. The stronger and more fit you are, the better you are able to withstand the impact of altitude. Altitude makes you work harder for less performance making you more fatigued with fewer miles than running at low altitude. So being strong and fit is even more important than it is in running at low altitudes where talent and specific running training relate to performance.

- The affects of running at altitude compound over the time. Fatigue from effort at altitude occurs earlier than fatigue from running at lower altitude levels because the effort to move at altitude is greater.
- There are metabolisms that physiologically perform easier at altitude and runners who have these metabolisms may train at altitude more readily and reap better than average results because of their metabolisms. These metabolisms have lungs with a residual lung capacity that holds a higher volume of the oxygen that is ordinarily exhaled by those with normal residual lung capacity. Runners with higher residual lung capacity use the "retained" oxygen for their running muscles so they are not as oxygen deprived and fatigued by their effort at altitude.

12.3 Knowing Altitude Sickness Symptoms

Crewing the climb up Mt Whitney requires a different set of "medical" skills than those used when crewing the runner in the heat of Death Valley. The runner who is fatigued, weakened, and spent from his/her effort in the Death Valley ultra can be more susceptible to altitude effects. Crew need to know and be able to recognize symptoms of altitude sickness in the runner and crew and know how to treat them. Here are classes of altitude sickness with symptoms and treatments.

Acute Mountain Sickness (AMS) generally occurs above 10,000'. Symptoms of AMS, vary by individual and are not related to age or physical condition. Aspirin taken when symptoms occur or herbal supplements compounded for altitude affects such as the all-natural ingredient Altitude Adjustment available at www.runningdelightis.com improve oxygen utilization while maximizing energy for athletic performance in high altitude. Such products taken before the start of the climb may be helpful. The definitive "cure" for altitude sickness is to go to lower elevation. After a nap where the altitude sick suffer sleeps deeply, the symptoms are relieved. Here are the symptoms of AMS that should be monitored to ensure that they do not escalate to High Altitude Pulmonary Edema (HAPES).

- Headache, nausea, and loss of appetite
- Dizziness, fatigue, and yawning
- Irregular breathing or shortness of breath
- Anxiety
- Hallucinations
- Slurred speech
- Unsteadiness

- Cyanosis (blue-tinged lips and tongues)

HAPES is a serious condition in which the lungs fill with fluid and can result in death if not treated promptly. HAPES symptoms include:

- Severe, persistent cough
- Rapid pulse over 110 per minute
- Rapid breathing over 20 per minute
- Gurgling chest sounds
- Confusion, delirium, irrational behavior

High Altitude Cerebral Edema (HACES) is a less common and more serious form of altitude sickness involves a swelling of the brain generally occurring when the victim has spent days above 12,000'. In addition to the symptoms of AMS and HAPES, HACES sufferers loose coordination.

For both HAPES and HACES descent to a lower altitude immediately. These conditions worsen during the night, so once determined, do not wait till morning to descend. An elevation of 2,000' or 3,000' lower can provide relief. It is not recommended to continue to climb when the victim improves. Severe cases should seek medical attention to avoid complications.

12.4 Preparing To Climb Mt Whitney

Having the fitness and training to complete a Death Valley ultra and then summit Mt Whitney demonstrates a special athlete and crew. Although climbing Mt Whitney can be a refreshing change from the heat of Death Valley and the simple hiking trail is not demanding, climbing Mt Whitney after running 135 miles in the desert a few hours earlier is challenging. To minimize the challenges of climbing Mt Whitney, perform the following tasks to prepare for the climb.

- Realistically **plan the amount of time** you expect to be one the mountain based on the runners condition — primarily the condition of his/her feet after the ultra and altitude training. Include time for bad weather. Although the Mt Whitney trail is an easy hiking trail, weather can slow down the hike to the summit or the descent. Realize that the distance to the summit is 6,200' over 11 miles and the same distance and elevation change on the return. Regular hikers are advised to take 2 days to do this climb. Most runners can walk up and down the Mt Whitney trail in about 15 hours excluding any problems.
- **Leave the trailhead before dawn** to return to the Mt Whitney Portal parking lot slightly after dark for the best use of light on the trail.

- **Plan nutrition** that can be conveniently carried on the trail for the crew and the runner for the number of hours you will be on the mountain. Take easy trail snack food such as nutrition bars, trail mix, and dried fruit removed from original packaging and double bagged in zip-lock baggies. Don't take fresh fruit that will bruise and squish in a pack. Sandwiches can be more effort than they are worth but if a crew member is willing to make them, they can be consumed at the first major nutrition stop on the hike up. Sandwiches squish easily in the pack.
- **Divide the runner's gear, nutrition, and water among the crew members' packs.** Designate one crew member to carry each category of items rather than distributing portions of items among crew member's packs. Avoid gloves in one crew member's pack, a hat in another pack, and wind pants in another.

Don'ts for Climbing Mt Whitney

- Don't leave the trailhead without lighting and backup lighting.
- Don't pass the lake at Trail Camp without filtering drinking water for all crew members' bladders.
- Don't separate.
- Don't leave food or other items with scents to attract bear to the crew van parked at the Mt Whitney trailhead parking lot.
- Don't use iodine or chlorine type water purification tablets. They take 30 minutes to activate in the cold water available on Whitney and you cannot use powdered drink mix in any bladder or bottle with these tablets.
- Don't forget sun protection when starting the climb in the dark. High altitude UV light and glare can affect performance and health.

- **Use electrolytes** on the mountain. It is a much cooler temperature but you will still be working and processing fluid for at least 10 hours.
- **Bring headlamps with fresh batteries and back up lighting** for all crew members and the runner. Batteries drain in extremely cold temperatures that can occur in bad weather high on the mountain. A micro photon light can provide light to replace batteries in the dark.

- Use at least a **70-ounce bladder and daypack water carry system with one water bottle for each crew member**. The water bottle may be useful when pumping filtered water from the lake and it is the runner's source for water. Crew members will carry the runner's water in bottles and hand the bottle to the runner periodically during the summit and descent.
- **Plan mountaineering clothing** which can be difficult to imagine after baking in the desert for days. Even though the pre-dawn start at 8,360' can be comparatively chilly, most hikers start in shorts as it warms up to avoid the time it takes to change into shorts on the trail. Pants with zip off legs can be a quick alternative providing both long pants and shorts in a single item. Carry a full set of light-weight, technical clothes to use for high-altitude bad weather for the runner and each crew member.
- **Affix the Mt Whitney permit cards to the back of each pack** with the self-attached wire ties in a location that prevents the card from blowing/slapping into faces in high winds.
- **Bring trekking poles for the fatigued runner** with sore feet and legs as the poles make it easier for runners to navigate the rocks and boulders on the trail.
- **Learn the trail**. After Trail Crest at mile 9, do not take the descending John Muir Trail. Realize that you summit Whitney from the west not the east, the orientation that you have viewed during the Death Valley ultra as the runner approached Lone Pine. Since the actual summit is difficult to see and the last mile to the summit can be covered with snow, it can be difficult find the route to the summit, particularly in low-clouds or snow showers or storms. On the descent with less than 3 miles to the trailhead, avoid accidentally taking the fork to Lone Pine Lake, especially in the dark.
- **Understand high altitude weather**. Weather at altitude can change very quickly. Bright, clear, warm weather can quickly turn into dangerous lighting strikes and no visibility.
- **Take any altitude medications** that may be necessary.

12.5 Crewing On Mt Whitney

Summiting a 14,000' mountain is a wonderful, lifetime experience and summiting Mt Whitney, the highest point in the continental United States after the contrast of running through the second hottest desert on the planet is a contrast of significant athletic ability. Here are considerations to make the last 22 miles of the Death Valley ultra successful.

- **Use the lake at Trail Camp to re-supply water**. The lake at mile 6.3 on the climb is close to the trail and does not take time to access. It is the easiest place to pump water as it is protected from wind and has a convenient shore line to spread out gear. After this point you will be without water for one half — the 10 top miles of the mountain (over 5 miles up and 5 miles back to the lake.) Fill all crew members' water bladders and bottles with filtered water from the lake at Trail Camp on the climb and on the descent. Do not pass through Trail Camp on the descent without filling all crew members' bladders even when everyone may be healthy and anticipate a quick completion. On the descent circumstances can happen below Trail Camp that can significantly increase the time to completion leaving you without sufficient water.
- For **emergency water sources, pump water from melting snow runoff.** These runoffs are on the trail but are just slightly above the lake. These source is more difficult to access and don't occur until you are nearly at the lake. Depending on the amount of snow and temperature, they may not exist in a particular year.
- **Record the runner's summit in the log at the summit of Mt Whitney**. Identify that the runner completed a 135-mile Death Valley ultra and his/her ultra time. Photograph the runner at the summit with the crew.
- **Be patient** with the Mt Whitney portion of the Death Valley ultra and stay together. Do not split up due to the conditions of team members. If a team member isn't healthy at a point on the climb, get him/her recovered, ideally while moving. Resting on the mountain can be dangerous as weather changes and effects of altitude can set in. Also, resting climber can become stiff and cold.
- **Add clothing** as temperatures and weather changes as you climb.
- **Use the waste and hygiene package** that comes with the permit when necessary on the trail.

That's when it struck me that the Quad had very little to do with me. It was for the starving children, for my dedicated crew, for the people who set foot in this desert with great appreciation, and for everyone that demands a better, more compassionate world to live in.

-- Marshall Ulrich, Badwater Quad Record Holder on his motivation for completing his record four crossings of Death Valley to Mt Whitney

Crewing For Mt Whitney

Appendix A — Conversions

This guide is written primarily in U.S. units of measure. For runners and crew who use metric units, this conversion appendix provides information to convert the units. For a calculator to convert the units of measure used in this guide go to http://www.chemie.fu-berlin.de/chemistry/general/units_en.html or use other similar unit converters. Use Table A as a quick reference for temperature conversions from Fahrenheit to Celsius.

Table A — Temperature Conversion

Degree Fahrenheit	Degree Celsius
89.6	32
91.4	33
93.2	34
95.0	35
96.8	36
98.6	37
100.4	38
102.2	39
104.0	40
105.8	41
107.6	42
109.4	43
111.2	44
113.0	45
114.8	46
116.6	47
118.4	48
120.2	49
122.0	50
123.8	51
125.6	52
127.4	53
128.4	54
130.2	55
132.0	56
133.8	57
135.6	58

Appendix B — Humorous Writings of Ben Jones

To provide comic relief to some of the serious health topics encountered at a Death Valley ultra, subjects, "Badwater Mayor" Ben Jones has experience practicing medicine in Death Valley for over three decades and participating in Death Valley ultras as a competitor, observer, advisor, consultant, and ambassador. Ben is in a good position to provide his humorous perspectives in the following short essays:

- Staying Subbarf At A Death Valley Ultra
- Staying Sub-Blister At A Death Valley Ultra

Staying Subbarf At A Death Valley Ultra

I have picked up a bit of terminology from a good biking friend John Hughes, Editor of UltraCycling. In one of his articles he used the expression "subbarf." I would like to introduce the term to the ultrarunning world as the subject "comes up" fairly frequently. I have even added some subcategories for assisting the runner in choosing his or her own anticipated barf level. I have included recommendations for handling the disorder. I have had some major input, or should I say "output," from USMC Major William Curt Maples, a Death Valley ultra participant since 1996. I have patterned much of this ultrarunning subbarf information after his spectacular regurgitations.

One of the keynote issues in a Death Valley ultra is "barfing." Most want to avoid it and others seem to revel in it and want to get it out of the way. This following list describes factions of this disorder as are made known.

#	Category	Description	Recommendations
1	SubBarf	Avoiding throwing up	Goal at a Death Valley ultra
2	PreBarf	Before throwing up	Let it go
3	PostBarf	After throwing up	Consider IVs but no DNF
4	MegaBarf	Large volume barf	Need trash barrel
5	GigaBarf	Larger volume barf	Need dumpster
6	MicroBarf	Teeny barfs	Need small zip-lock baggie
7	MiniBarf	Small barfs	Need medium zip-lock baggie
8	MarcoBarf	Large barfs	Need large zip-lock baggie
9	NanoBarfs	Very small barfs	Use Kleenex
10	PicoBarfs	Even smaller barfs	Use blotter
11	PseudoBarfs	Fake vomiting	See psychiatrist except for media coverage performances
12	Barfosis	Vomiting syndrome	Needs MD clearance
13	Barfosis Imperfecta	Faulty barfing	Needs improvement and more adaptation
14	BarfoPhobia	Fear of barfing	Prerequisite for official Death Valley ultra
15	BarfoPhilia	Enjoying barfing	Not recommended
16	BarfoThon	Vomiting event	Check with official event headquarters
17	BarfoRama	Also vomiting event	Same as for the -Thon
18	BarfoLalia	Repetitive barfing	Alert the media
19	SupraBarf	Maintaining barfing level	Request paramedics and the media

#	Category	Description	Recommendations
20	InfraBarf	Failing to achieve barf level	Not ready for prime time
21	HyperBarf	Same as macro barf	Refer to Marco
22	HypoBarf	Same as micro barf	Refer to Mini
23	OmniBarf	All round barfing	Needs more acclimatization
24	NormoBarf	Normal vomiting	Misconception

Staying Sub-Blister At A Death Valley Ultra

Normal people would not even consider running a Death Valley ultra. In case you think you might want to, here is some information to help you be successful, preventing blisters, an important factor in a Death Valley ultra's success.

I am using the newly coined term "subblister" which is a spin off of "subbarf." I picked up the later term from a biking friend and felt compelled to introduce both terms to the ultrarunning world. The "subbarf" essay had already been published and received some remarkable rave reviews. I have borrowed some terms from the medical profession, as you will be able to tell in the categories that I developed in the following list.

Along with the types of blisters is a vivid description of the different kinds of blisters that can be encountered even before reaching Furnace Creek Ranch at the 17-mile mark on the Death Valley ultra course. There is an even better prospect of witnessing these blister disorders occurring aat a Death Valley ultra as the ultra progresses at locations near the Salt Creek turnoff (30 miles) and the Devil's Cornfield (35 miles). Theses locations are the so-called BlisteroThon in earlier stages of blister disorder. For some, the final stage known as the BlisteroRama, a spectacular festival or even carnival depending on the number of attendees and the magnitude of the blisters, occurs at Stovepipe Wells Village at 41 miles.

#	Category*	Description	Recommendations
1	SubBlister	Avoiding blisters	Goal at a Death Valley ultra
2	Blisterosis	Blister syndrome	Avoid
3	PreBlisterosis	Impending blistering	Back off-stop and tape
4	PostBlisterosis	No-Pay-Attention	Should have listened
5	BlisteroMania	Blistering psychosis	See psychologist and get counseling
6	BlisteroPhobia	Fear of blistering	Prerequisite for a Death Valley ultra
7	BlisteroPhilia	Desire of blistering	Not recommended
8	Blisterosis Imperfecta	Imperfect blistering	Needs more foot taping practice or use duct tape
9	HyperBlisterosis	Extreme capacity for blistering	Needs a lot of bandages and needles
10	MacroBlisterosis	Ditto	Ditto
11	HypoBlisterosis	Reduced capacity for blistering	Don't pre-tape feet and don't wear socks
12	MicroBlisterosis	Infinitesimal capacity to not blister	Death Valley has been berry, berry good to me
13	MegaBlisterosis	Large blisters	Use minipads
14	GigaBlisterosis	Very large blisters	Use maxipads
15	MiniBlisterosis	Small blister disorder	Use Micropore tape
16	NanoBlisterosis	Smaller blisters	Think about taping

Pace Chart

#	Category*	Description	Recommendations
17	PicoBlisterosis	Even smaller blisters	Leave alone
18	BlisterOthon	Event producing blisters	Witness phenomenon en route
19	BlisterOrama	Blister festival or carnival	Attend ceremony at Stovepipe Wells
20	Blisterosis pigmentosa	Pigmented blisters; calico effect	Use air brush
21	Melanotic Blisterosis	Black blisters	Chemotherapy or irradiation therapy
22	Purpuric blisterosis	Bruised blisters	Return to the Badwater pond and restart
23	Blisterosis Sanguinosa	Ditto	Ditto
24	Hyperkeratotic Blisterosis	Scaly, thickened blisters	Dermabrasion
25	Bullous Blisterosis	Bubble-shaped blisters	Open and drain – use tub
26	PseudoBlisterosis	Fake blisters	Okay for media coverage
27	Blisterosis verde aka Pseudomonas Blisterosis	Green blisters	IV Vancomycin
28	Blisterosis Gangrenosa	Gangrenous blisters	Amputation
29	SupraBlisterosis	Maintaining high blister count	Enter on the “Richter” scale of blistering
30	InfraBlisterosis	Inability to develop blisters	Desired for a Death Valley ultra
30	OmniBlisterosis	Blisters on both feet and all toes	Alert the media
31	BlisteroLalia	Recurrent blistering	Attend Denise Jones’ blister clinics
32	Blisterosis Sicca	Dry blisters	Use Hydropel
33	Blisterosis Deformans	Awkward blisters	Use reshaping device
34	Pemphigoid Blisterosis	Bubbly blisters	Get out syringe
35	Macular Blisterosis	Red blisters	Use SPF cream
36	Papular Blisterosis	Bumpy blisters	Dermabrasion as in #24
37	Blisterosis Migrans	Wandering blisters	Don’t confuse with parasitic larvae

Appendix C — Death Valley Ultra Pace Chart

Prepared by Ben Jones

Miles to finish

	35	34	33	32	31	30	29	28	27	26	25	24	23	22	21	20	19
36																	
35	60:00																
34	58:17	60:00															
33	56:34	58:14	60:00														
32	54:52	56:28	58:11	60:00													
31	53:09	54:43	56:22	58:08	60:00												
30	51:25	52:56	54:33	56:15	58:04	60:00											
29	49:43	51:11	52:43	54:23	56:08	58:00	60:00										
28	48:00	49:25	50:55	52:30	54:11	56:00	57:56	60:00									
27	46:17	47:40	49:05	50:37	52:16	54:00	55:52	57:52	60:00								
26	44:34	45:53	47:16	48:45	50:19	52:00	53:47	55:43	57:47	60:00							
25	42:51	41:04	45:27	46:53	43:23	50:00	51:43	53:34	55:34	57:41	60:00						
24	41:08	42:21	43:38	45:00	46:27	48:00	49:40	51:26	53:20	55:23	57:36	60:00					
23	39:26	40:35	41:49	43:78	44:31	46:00	47:35	49:17	51:06	53:04	55:12	57:30					
22	37:42	38:49	40:00	41:15	42:35	44:00	45:31	47:08	48:53	50:46	52:48	55:00	60:00				
21	36:00	37:04	38:11	39:23	40:39	42:00	43:27	45:00	46:40	48:28	50:24	52:30	57:23	60:00			
20	34:17	35:17	36:22	37:30	38:43	40:00	41:23	42:52	44:26	46.09	48:00	50:00	54:47	57:16	60:00		
19	32:34	33:32	34:33	35:38	36:46	38:00	39:19	40:43	42:13	43:51	45:36	47:30	52:10	54:33	57:08	60:00	
18	30:52	31:46	32:44	33:45	34:50	36:00	37:14	38:34	40:00	41:32	43:12	45:00	49:34	51:49	54:17	57:00	60:00
17	29:08	30:00	30:55	31:53	32:54	34:00	35:10	36:26	37:47	39:14	40:48	42:30	46:58	49:05	51:26	54:00	56:50
16	27:26	28:14	29:54	30:00	30:58	32:00	33:06	34:17	35:34	39:56	38:24	40:00	44:21	46:22	48:34	51:00	53:41
15	25:43	26:28	27:16	28:08	29:02	30:00	31:02	32:08	33:20	34:37	36:00	37:30	41:44	43:38	45:43	48:00	50:32
14	24:00	24:43	25:27	26:15	27:06	28.00	28:58	30:00	31:07	32:19	33:36	35:00	39:08	40:55	42:52	45:00	47:22
13	22:17	22:56	23:38	24:23	25:10	26:00	29:54	27:52	28:53	30:00	31:12	32:30	36:31	38:11	40:00	42:00	44:13
12	20:34	21:11	21:49	22:30	23:14	24:00	24:50	25:43	26:40	27:41	28:48	30:00	33:55	35:27	37:08	39:00	41:03
11	18:52	19:25	20:00	20:38	21:17	22:00	22:46	23:34	24:26	25:23	26:24	27:30	31:18	32:44	34:17	36:00	37:53
10	17:08	17:04	18:11	18:45	19:21	20:00	20:41	21:26	22:13	23:05	24:00	25:00	28:42	30:00	31:26	33:00	34:44
09	15:26	15:32	16:22	16:53	17:26	18:00	18:37	19:17	20:00	20:46	21:36	22:30	26:05	27:16	28:34	30:00	31:35
08	13:43	14:07	14:33	15:00	15:29	16:00	16:33	17:08	17:47	18:28	19:07	20:00	23:29	24:33	25:43	27:00	28:25
07	12:00	12:12	12:44	13:08	13:33	14:00	14:29	15:00	15:34	16:10	16:48	17:30	20:52	21:49	22:52	24:00	25:16
06	10:10	10:35	10:55	11:15	11:10	12:00	12:25	12:52	13:20	13:51	14:24	15:00	18:16	19:05	20:00	21:00	22:07
05						10:00	10:20	10:43	11:07	11:32	12:00	12:30	15:39	16:22	17:08	18:00	18:57
04											09:36	10:00	13:02	13:38	14:17	15:00	15:47
03													10:26	10:55	11:26	12:00	12:38
02																	
01																	
Hours to a 60-Hr finish																	

Pace Chart

18	17	16	15	14	13	12	11	10	9	8	7	6	5	4	3	2	1
60:00																	
56:40	60:00																
53:20	56:28	60:00															
50:00	52:56	56:15	60:00														
46:40	49:25	52:30	56:00	60:00													
43:20	45:53	48:45	52:00	55:43	60:00												
40:00	42:21	45:00	48:00	51:26	55:23	60:00											
36:40	38:49	41:15	44:00	47:08	50:46	55:00											
33:20	35:17	37:30	40:00	42:52	46:09	50:00	60:00										
30:00	31:46	33:45	36:00	38:34	41:32	45:00	54:33	60:00									
26:40	28:14	30:00	32:00	34:17	36:55	40:00	49:05	54:00	60:00								
23:20	24:43	26:15	28:00	30:00	32:19	35:00	43:38	48:00	53:20	60:00							
20:00	21:11	22:30	24:00	25:43	27:41	30:00	38:11	42:00	46:40	52:30	60:00						
16:40	17:39	18:45	20:00	21:26	23:05	25:00	32:44	36:00	40:00	45:00	51:26	60					
13:20	14:07	15:00	16:00	17:08	18:28	20:00	27:16	30:00	33:20	37:30	42:52	50	60				
10:00	10:35	11:15	12:00	12:52	13:05	15:00	41:49	24:00	26:40	30:00	34:17	40	48	60			
						10:00	16:22	18:00	20:00	22:30	25:43	30	36	45	60		
							10:55	12:00	13:20	15:00	17:08	20	24	30	40	60	
							05:27	*06:00*	*06:40*	*07:30*	*08:34*	10	12	15	20	30	60
							It's difficult to run the last 11 mi. on the Portal Road in 1 hr. at a rate of 5:27. These paces are unrealistic.										

Pace Chart

Bibliography

Endurance Sports Nutrition: Eating plans for optimal training, racing, and recovery by Suzanne Girard Eberle, MS, RD, Human Kenetics, 2000.

Exertional Heat Illnesses by Lawrence E. Armstrong. 2003. Human Kinetics Publishers.

Fixing Your Feet: Prevention and Treatments for Athletes by John Vonhof. Wilderness Press; 3rd edition (June 15, 2004) www.fixingyourfeet.com.

Lore of Running by Tim Nokes, MD. Human Kinetics Publishers. 4th edition. 2002.

Running Badwater by Mike Henebry posted to the ultralist May 2005.

Running on the Sun DVD, Rhino home video, by Mel Stuart, 2000.

The Death Valley 300: Near Death and Resurrection on the World's Toughest Endurance Course by Rich Benyo. Specific Pubns. 1991.

To the Edge: A Man, Death Valley, and the Mystery of Endurance by Kirk Johnson. Warner Books. 2001.